# The Demarcation Line

# The Demarcation Line

## a Memoir

Fernande Wagman

This book was printed in the United States of America.

**To order additional copies of this book, contact:**
Xlibris Corporation
1-888-795-4274
www.Xlibris.com
Orders@Xlibris.com
19563

# Contents

I extend my heartelt appreciation to my husband, Edward,
whose continued support and advice were essential to the
completion of this story of survival

\*   \*   \*

This volume is dedicated to:

Deborah and Rami, Vera and Russell, Marc-David and Felice
and
Aryeh, Daniel, Sarah, and Alexandra
with love and affection
and
to the French Christians who saved us.

# PREFACE

This book is the recorded recollections of my dear wife of fifty years.

They concentrate particularly on that early period of her life, from 1939 to 1953, during the Nazi occupation of France and its aftermath. This memoir is reminiscent of many others concerning this horrific period of world history, which has become known as the Holocaust. Yet, in my opinion, each story of this era is highly personal, and even perhaps unique, in its own right.

The research that my wife and I carried out took us to the Jewish museum and other locations in Paris, to the archives in Aix-les-Bains and Chambéry, and visits to Yenne, Izieu and small villages in the foothills of the Alps. It is inconceivable that such terrifying events could occur in such beautiful and serene surroundings, and yet they did. For me, it was an enlightening and too often a devastating experience.

I am most proud of Fernande, my closest friend and companion, for her many accomplishments, and particularly for her determination and fortitude in preparing this memoir. It required that she relive a very threatening and stressful period of her life, to help further assure that the Holocaust is not forgotten.

Edward Wagman, M.D.—May 2003

# CHAPTER I

## THE DEMARCATION LINE

I did Hitler in, on many an occasion, in my dreams, with a sharp kitchen knife, after climbing through his bedroom window. It was always the same dream. No blood was spilled. I always came through triumphant and was never caught. While this may have fulfilled a subconscious need, it clearly did not have the desired effect, nor did Mother's varied and colorful Yiddish curses. On any pretext, she would yell, "A kapore af Hitlerin," "A chalerea af Hitlerin," "Soll Hitler gehen in drerd," "Soll er veren geharget," "A rak soll ihm nehmen," wishing Hitler a painful death by cholera, cancer, or physical violence. Hitler seemed to be impervious to it all.

The news of Grandmother's death deepened my subconscious feeling of anxiety. On returning from school one day, Maman was in bed, crying, with red and swollen eyes, a letter from Kedaniai, the *shtetl* (little village) in Lithuania, in hand. With a gentle consoling kiss and embrace I asked, "Why did Grandma die?" "A *rak!*" was the curt answer. Childish imagination caused me to consider that a *rak* was a sort of black beast with tentacles invading the body and killing it but later discovered that it meant cancer in Yiddish. My imagination was, after all, not far from the truth.

Hitler was our *rak*.

The night frightened me. I frequently awakened in the throes of a nightmare, screaming in terror, a monster invariably in pursuit.

Papa would carry me through the entire apartment to assure that no creature was anywhere in hiding. I ended up sleeping between my parents.

Night still frightens me, when it appears that most unpleasant events occur.

This certainly did happen one night in May 1941.

Uncle Isaac had arrived from Germany via Belgium where his wife, Aunt Rosa, one of father's sisters, had remained. I liked my uncle Isaac, who spoke in soft, soothing Yiddish laced with German, smiling as he proudly told me of his two sons, Zigi and Sami, who had already gone to Palestine and enlisted in the British Army. Their photographs revealed good-looking young men in military uniform.

This evening, in my crib (although I am nine years old), I have trouble falling asleep while listening to the nightly parental arguments—whether or not to leave Paris. The German edict that Jewish businesses must be administered by Gentiles is another humiliation for the French Jews (adding to the growing list). Papa and Max Ochsman, his partner, have agreed to appoint Claude Magnin, Max's son-in-law who is Christian, to this position. Tonton Isaac repeats the rumors of concentration camps in Germany, similar to those in France, in Pithiviers and Drancy. The window curtains are drawn, and it is pitch black in the room. Not comprehending the discussion, the total darkness increases my discomfort. *Will monsters grab me and take me away from Papa and Maman? Where to? What are concentration camps? Don't think. Don't talk. Watch out for the concierge, that* pipelette (gossip), *who likes to converse with the tenants.* The walls have ears. *People can denounce you. What does it mean, denounce? Papa and Maman should cease their conversation.* Finally, Uncle Isaac bids farewell and leaves for the neighboring hotel. A sigh of relief escapes me. In the dark, Papa and Maman slip into bed, which is next to my crib. It is cozy, quiet, and relaxing. Sleep finally comes.

Suddenly, startling bright lights awaken me. I am abruptly attentive to the surroundings. It is the middle of the night and dark outside. No sounds, except for labored breathing. At the bedroom door are two French policemen in trench coats with Uncle Isaac, Maman, Papa, and Mania, my mother's cousin, nearby, quivering with cold and fear, their faces as white as bedsheets. Now really frightened, I get cramps and hold my tummy. *What is going on?*

"Vos papiers." Papa is asked for his papers.

"What did we do?" says my father, fumbling for them in the desk's drawer, and then handing them over, trembling, to the policemen.

"Your brother-in-law provided this address because he left some clothing here. We are taking him away." No signs of sympathy or reassuring smile are reflected on the impassive faces of the policemen. Their blank stares are chilling. We tremble.

"We did not do anything," murmurs my father.

"Well, we have our duty."

"I have been in France for many years, and I love this country. *Je suis Français*," declares Papa in a husky voice, "and truly, I don't understand this."

Uncle Isaac asks permission to go to the bathroom and is followed by one of the policemen. Maman, in the meantime, gathers the clothes in a rage and, when Isaac comes out of the WC, glares at him. *Why did he bring the police to our apartment and put us in jeopardy?* Later, she tells us of barely controlling the urge to give him *a setz* (a blow he would remember). Maman, flushing, throws the garments in his face and yells, "Geh in drerd" (literally, "go to the earth!"; "die!"). "Kum hier nicht mehr" (don't ever come here again).

To this day, it is not readily understandable why these policemen spare us. Perhaps, we are not included on the "list," or maybe they are just cops doing a distasteful job. They say good night, as if nothing has happened, and take Uncle Isaac along. I don't recall sleeping that night. My parents and Mania are still pale and shaking, trying to decide what to do. It is definitely a signal to leave Paris.

Frantically, the next day, Papa makes arrangements for

Maman, Mania, and me to flee immediately for the Unoccupied Zone. Papa will come later, wanting to remain in Paris to settle his affairs with Max and Claude, who is taking over the factory by order of the authorities. Many Jews are going to Aix-Les-Bains, to the Savoie, in the Alps, near Italy. (1)

French Jews, including my father, are incredibly naïve, and falsely optimistic, believing that Southeast France is far from German subjugation, and where the occupying Italians are refuted to be more lenient to the Jews. Further, entrée into "neutral" Switzerland is thought to be possible (*little did we know!*). Maman and Mania begin to pack, which includes removing hidden valuables from the bedroom wall. Gold coins, American dollars, and jewels are sewn into the lining of coats; French money is hidden in the soles of our shoes.

A few days after the incident with Tonton Isaac, my uncle has the audacity to return to the apartment. Papa is not at home. Maman is about to throw him out but does not have the physical strength to do so and is also curious as to what happened, while cursing him in very colorful, quite vulgar Russian. Isaac calmly relates that he was fortunate not to have been sent to the labor camps in Germany or Poland. At the interrogation station, there were two lines of people, one going to the camps and the other returning home. Unbelievably, he was released because he wore spectacles and could not be useful to the Germans (*or so they apparently thought*). Isaac apologizes. Maman, after initially exploding, cannot remain angry for any length of time and forgives him. They kiss, wishing each other *Mazel* (luck), and I kiss him too.

The next day he returned to Belgium, and we lost contact until the end of the war.

While preparing for our departure, Papa was concerned because the Demarcation Line, which separated the occupied and unoccupied zones, had to be crossed. This Demarcation Line was, of all the evidence of German power, the most annoying and humbling (2) to the French people. The Nazis used it as a means for political pressure, opening and closing it at will. Geographically, it isolated two vastly different regions in France: the primarily industrial North (wheat, coal, and iron production), including Paris, and the agricultural South with its vineyards and large cities (Lyon, Marseille, Bordeaux). It was disheartening to wait on lengthy lines to obtain an *Ausweis* or permit to pass the frontier, for which only emergency situations were acceptable. (2)

Trains were stopped at the border, where Nazi agents in civilian clothes would check for proper documents. This was especially dangerous for the Jews, who were most at risk. *Passeurs* were individuals willing to take people or merchandise for money, into the Free Zone. Their fee would vary with the degree of risk.

Although his wife remained with him in Paris, Claude Magnin wanted his mother-in-law, Anale Ochsman, to leave the Occupied Zone, which was more hazardous. Max, her husband, would join her later. Claude arranged everything.

I recall the drive in his car. Mania is sitting in the front near Claude. Being small for my age, I am squashed between Maman and Anale. The cold penetrates my body, and I feel paralyzed with fear of the unknown. Although the two women try to keep me calm and warm, I cannot help shivering. Lulled by the droning sound of the motor, I fall asleep. Our destination is Vierzon, a small town on the Cher River, a tributary of the Loire. We arrive in the evening. It is already dark. A chill wind is blowing. The curfew has everyone at home, their curtains drawn. Claude has engaged four *passeurs* who work in the Occupied Zone and live in the Free Zone.

They already have permits to take us across the Demarcation Line. Anale, Mania, and Maman are supposedly the wives of three of these men, and I, the child of the fourth. At the border, there is a long line of people, some with bikes. They advance slowly, silent and grim. It is bitter cold. The German soldiers examine the documents and permits. Some people are held over, some pass quickly. Mania, Anale, and Maman go safely through the checkpoint. Now, it is my turn. My *passeur* repeats the admonitions I have heard previously, many times, "Don't forget! You are supposed to be my little girl. Do not say a word; I'll do all

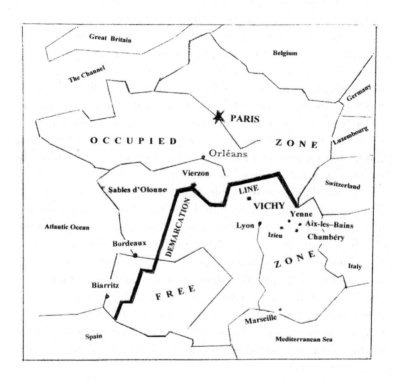

Map of France during the Occupation

the talking. You are tiny enough, and I'll hold you in my arms. Don't forget to call me Papa!" Although I am very young, the danger is apparent to me. It is instinctive. Only children below eight years can "pass" with their father. I have to play the part, knowing that le Boche (derogatory word for the German) is going to hurt me if I am not quiet. My arms are curled around the passeur's neck, with my head partly concealed by his shoulder. As he approaches the checkpoint, I dare not look at the German soldier. My heart is beating faster and faster, I can hear it, slamming against my ribs, and don't feel the cold anymore.

A bark: "Papieren!"

The guard takes a sharp look at the Ausweis, glances at us, then back at the paper. Grimacing, he shows it to his companion and speaks German. Hey! It sounds like Yiddish. I can understand what he says, "I bet this child is not his daughter. I think we have a phony here." Raising my head, at that moment, looking at my mother, waiting safely at the other side of the border, I can see that she senses something is amiss and starts to move back towards me, pale, with open mouth, ready to cry out. On impulse, I turn to my surrogate "father," whining in French, "Papa, qu'est-ce qu'il dit le monsieur? Je veux rentrer à la maison" (Papa, what does this man say? I want to go home). The German hears me say "Papa." He gives us a hard look, scans my "father's" papers once again, and reluctantly, it seems, mutters, "Passez!" Maman starts to approach but, seeing us pass the border, stops, smiles, and manages to control the urge to press me tightly in her arms, which she proceeds to do, as soon as we are safely settled in a small hotel.

Total darkness still makes me uncomfortable. Sleep eludes me, and my concerns seem to amplify. Curtains are never totally drawn. Any light from without, especially the moon, is reassuring. Sometimes, during a sleepless night, my eyes don't close until dawn, when the sun rises, and all seems tranquil again.

I was ten years old when this story was first written as an assignment at school in the Savoie. The teacher wanted the pupils to relate a "misadventure." Madame Moliaix gave me an A for this "terrorizing experience" and read it aloud to a class of *petits paysans* who understandably could not appreciate its full meaning. The so-called Free Zone, or as some called it *la zone nono* (an abbreviated form for *la zone non occupée*) eventually, also became "occupied." The French Milice aided the SS in capturing Jews, but with even greater diligence and enthusiasm.

We had escaped twice.

As I get older, I believe more and more in fate. "It is *beschert!*" as my parents used to say. It was meant to be.

# CHAPTER II

## A SELF-MADE MAN

Throughout history, the Jews have been subjugated and slaughtered and yet remarkably have survived. When I was born in 1932, the world was already in turmoil. During the first six years of my life, Adolf Hitler was already placing together the early mechanism necessary to carry out the Final Solution. Of course I did not know this then.

My parents came from countries where anti-Semitism was an inherent part of the culture. In Russia, the tsars were often the leading anti-Semites. The procurator of the Saint-Synode of the Orthodox Church predicted that one-third of the Jews would perish, one-third would leave the land, and one-third would assimilate. This belief helped facilitate the persecution and the organized, often fatal attacks on Jews, called pogroms, which were carried out by the peasantry and Cossacks, under the passive observation of the police and army. (3)

During this period, similar events occurred in Poland, the country of my father's birth. He was the ninth child of a Polish rabbi, my grandfather Ephraim, my namesake. At the end of the First World War, Papa, at the age of nineteen, left Warsaw for Berlin, Germany. He showed great courage in leaving his beloved family and country, probably forever, speaking only Yiddish and Polish. Learning a new language and culture, he sought freedom but was disheartened and stifled by the terrible unemployment and inflation then prevalent in Germany. A loaf of bread cost thousands of marks, he said. My father remained in Germany for eight years and was witness to the political turmoil and the rise of Adolf Hitler. (4) Papa would often make jest of this obscure Austrian customs official's son, who, while dreaming of becoming a great artist, was reduced to being a housepainter instead. Then as a politician in post-World War I, he apparently never forgot the resentment of failed youthful ambitions. Papa also remembered the *Putsch* of 1923. Hitler, with the support of stormtroopers (Schutz-Abteilung), attempted unsuccessfully to take over the government, was arrested, and sent to Landsberg prison. " . . . where *Mein Kampf* (My Combat) was written, in which the Nazi philosophy was described." As Papa explained at the end of World War II, only then did the Jews belatedly, and many others, realize its full significance. (5)

My father had learned the leather-cutting trade in Berlin, which served him in good stead in later years. Observing the changing mood in Germany, he immigrated to France in 1928.

Once, I asked Papa if he regretted leaving Germany. "No, no, no. I am happy in France. The only good memory of Berlin is the time spent at the opera, and since money was in short supply, I would stand in the rear of the theater, listening. It was superb."

On his arrival in Paris, Papa was hired as a leather cutter in a factory. Most Jews who fled the pogroms from Eastern Europe were artisans, who worked in the fur, jewelry, furniture, and leather industries. Upward social mobility developed primarily in the second generation. Ambitious and frugal, Father was impatient to become independent, starting a shoe factory with a partner, Max Ochsman, in the late thirties.

After the separation of church and state in 1905, many Frenchmen felt that the Dreyfus Affair (6) which had received worldwide attention was then also concluded and must be forgotten. It was not. Anti-Semitism was rampant, and to avoid this prejudice, it was said that the Jews want to assimilate and forget their religion. (7) Many Jewish families made themselves as invisible as possible: "Shah! Shtill!" (Quiet!) *Don't flaunt your Jewishness! You are a Frenchman first!* As a new immigrant, Papa knew that the rank of *Israëlite*, the elite Jewish establishment who were born in France, was unattainable. He was a *Juif* and was going to assimilate but retain the traditions. He became fluent in the language and was also self-taught in French history. Papa enjoyed crude Gallic humor as well as the subtle wit of the *chansonniers* (comedians in the Mort Sahl and Dennis Miller style). He continued to speak Yiddish among family and friends, celebrating only Passover in family gatherings, but never went to the synagogue, even on the High Holy Days of Rosh Hashanah and Yom Kippur.

Papa once showed me a family picture. I recognized him immediately, standing behind his father, the patriarch, a venerable, bearded man with a *yarmulke* (skullcap), while his mother and sisters stood or sat nearby. As I write about my father, it seems that I am alone with him, having a visit. I thought details of his face, of his voice were forgotten after these many years, but old photographs help revive the memories. Papa had a balding, squarish head, softened by rounded features, punctuated by a bulbous nose, the result of an accident, with a rim of gray hair, glistening with Cadoricin. The commercial for this fashionable pomade would often be shown in the cinemas. A lovely woman would shake her mane of beautiful hair, with a smile and a joyous, "Bravo, Cadoricin!" Papa, imitating the model, would wiggle his bare head and make us laugh.

The shiny bald spot enlarged as years went on.

Papa smiled pleasantly but did not laugh very often. I guess he wanted to hide his teeth, which revealed years of neglect and tobacco stains. I inherited his twinkling hazel eyes. Papa grew a mustache, but Maman said it was reminiscent of Hitler's, and so it was removed. I enjoyed watching him shave in the morning, standing precariously on the *bidet*, and now still remember the scent of the aftershave lotion, spicy but subdued like him. He was small in stature but was a giant to me. A quiet man who

**Part of my father's family.**

Sitting from left to right: My grandfather, Ephraim; Aunt
    Régine, Fanny's mother; and my grandmother Ida.
Standing from left to right: Papa, Aunt Rosa, and two
    other aunts.
Children sitting: his nieces, Suzanne and Fanny (right)
Standing: Jeannette.

never raised his voice or ever struck me, a scowl was sufficient to
indicate dissatisfaction, and for me to obey. *Fifi* was my nickname.
To be called *Fernande* (a name that I intensely disliked) was
punishment for misbehavior! Maman could scream her head off
and would be ignored. My trust in him was complete. His presence
made me feel protected, safe, and strong. Conversely, my anxieties
were precipitated in his absence and worsened by Maman's
continued screeching. At night, only his reassurance could
dissipate my childhood fear. Although without formal education,
Papa seemed generally knowledgeable. His French was slightly
accented, and we conversed in this language. Maman usually

spoke Yiddish. Russian or Polish were used when the discussion was not for my ears (or so they thought). After a while, I intuitively understood the meaning of some words, such as *daye!* Russian for "capitulate!" That word meant success, because I usually got what I wanted. Relaxing in his leather slippers and dull brown wool housecoat, Papa enjoyed reading to me in the evening, with a snifter of cognac in his hand, while patiently listening to my interruptions.

"I love you, Papa. I am going to marry you when I am a big girl."

"You always say that, Fifi, *chérie*," he chuckled, "but that will change later, you will see."

"Jamais" (Never).

I staunchly promised him, with childish certitude, "Je le sais!" (I know it!) When I was young, he seemed immortal. The alternative was unthinkable. Yet now, much later, existence without him is bearable, as my life is so filled with love for my husband, children, and grandchildren.

Maman observed this special relationship with mixed emotions. Sometimes she would complain to my father, a martyred look on her face, "Du ost mir nicht lieb, nur dein tochter" (You don't love me, only your daughter). Her jealousy was so obvious that a divorce seemed imminent. *It was my fault. Maman was angry with me. Quick, quick! A hug and a kiss to reassure her.* I felt guilty loving my father so much.

Papa helped me appreciate books at an early age. They were magical and enhanced my life. The first stories read were by Madame la Comtesse de Ségur, a popular French author of children's books of the nineteenth century. Reading became one of my favorite pastimes, particularly on rainy days, seated in a comfortable chair. La Comtesse de Ségur's many tales were devoured, along with lots of chocolate. Her characters were of the aristocracy. I envied those privileged little girls who lived in palaces, had servants, addressed their parents with the formal *vous*, and were usually obedient. Their life was quite different from mine. Mothers didn't screech but spoke in refined, modulated tones.

Fairies were real to me. So was Père Noël, who had nothing to do with Christianity, as far as Papa and I were concerned. After all, we were now Frenchmen and acted accordingly. I firmly believed in the existence of this venerable, bearded man whose long monastic robe hid black boots. Excitedly, I wondered for days what my gifts would be and bombarded my parents with questions. They smiled knowingly and quietly. I was sure of a windfall and looked longingly at the chimney. On Christmas morning, my shoes, which had been put near the fireplace the night before, were filled with toys I had requested in my letter to Père Noël. Sleep was fitful on Christmas Eve. One such night, when I was six, I crept silently into the dining room. Imagine my extreme disappointment and sadness when I caught Papa placing a doll in the chimney. Named Solange, a Shirley Temple look-alike, the doll was as tall as I and became the symbol of my lost belief. Replacing a real friend, Solange had no expression and never argued, which was fine, since the disagreements with my mother were sufficient. Maman made her dresses and bows similar to mine. I told Solange of my fantasies and read her Madame de Ségur's wonderful fairy tales. Although belief in Père Noël was gone, they continued to bring joy to my life. Indeed, fairy tales have happy endings, and the wicked are punished. Princes and princesses are beautiful, and love always wins out. Everything is predictable and therefore, safe. A fairy tale is an ideal world where effort is rewarded. During my adolescence, Papa enthusiastically repeated this encouragement to me: "You can do it." I grew up believing that "vouloir c'est pouvoir" (If you have the will, it can be done). Later in life, after a hard day's work, I would sigh with regret, missing the cat's claw (provided by a fairy) to rub on my forehead, erasing fatigue and signs of age. Ah! To live in this ideal world!

I felt secure and nurtured in a parental cocoon during early childhood, despite the threatening events in Europe of which I was not aware. It seems that loss of Père Noël heralded the end of the safe years before the war.

I kept Madame de Ségur's books, including my *Bibliothèque*

*Rose* in its dark pink hardcover these many years, despite the family's numerous relocations. My daughters loved these stories too. Often regretting not having learned Russian and Polish from my parents, I was determined not to repeat the same mistake. French was spoken to my children soon after they were born, and the stories of Madame de Ségur were read to them before bedtime, especially *Les Petites Filles Modèles*. The little girls described in the story remained so perfect. Their ideal existence now seemed outdated, and unrelated to my daughters' life or my own. However, Deborah and Vera hung on to every word, eyes shining, attentive, just as I had, as a little girl. "Maman, do not stop. Tell us more!"

Marc, my son, on the other hand, was interested in more manly stories.

Looking at my girls' rapt faces, I remembered Papa.

He would have liked to listen to us.

Perhaps he is!

# CHAPTER III

## EXASPERATING AND LOVABLE

Maman was the typical *Yiddishe Momme*, providing the usual remedies for colds such as chicken soup, or *goggle moggles,* consisting of hot milk, raw egg, and honey, for sore throat. She was obsessed with food, overfeeding dinner guests to the point of gluttony, encouraging them periodically to eat more, "Ess! Ess!"

The song "A Yiddishe Momme," made popular by Sophie Tucker, was a favorite. Head nodding, eyes brimming with tears, Maman sang in a lovely soprano:

"A *Yiddishe Momme, es gibt nit besser in der velt*" (A Jewish mom, there is none better in the world).

"A *Yiddishe Momme, oy, vay, vie bitter ven zie fehlt!*" (A Jewish mom, oh, how painful, how bitter when she dies!)

These lyrics conveyed to me a different message: "Don't you see how you treat me, you bad girl. Wait! You'll see when you'll lose me! You'll cry too!" Thinking it was great melodrama, I would walk away, smirking, but nevertheless with the intended feeling of guilt.

My *Yiddishe Momme.* You were funny, loving, and exasperating.

Maman was a very timid twenty-six-year-old spinster on arriving in the late 1920s in Paris, from Kedaniai, a small town in Lithuania, leaving behind a widowed mother and four siblings. (8) Maman's mother, Fanny, had married a lawyer, who was well regarded in the village. When he died of cholera, my grandmother tried to make ends meet as a seamstress, but the family was impoverished. To make matters worse, the Cossacks would periodically rampage through the town, killing those Jews in sight. After the Soviets occupied Lithuania, learning Russian was required in the schools. Regretfully, I am not more knowledgeable concerning this part of my mother's life, not having had the curiosity to ask, perhaps being subconsciously burdened by her pain, since all family members perished during the Holocaust. Recently, a television program dealt with the rise of socialism in Vilna, Lithuania's capital. I found this fascinating, and various questions came to mind. Had my family been politically involved? My grandmother Fanny might have been. Maman said that she was very intelligent.

Maman's given name was Vera. Since she did not understand French when arriving in Paris, she frequently heard the phrase: "on verra, on verra" (we'll see, we'll see!) and thought it referred to her. This made her very self-conscious. She came from Lithuania to Paris with the Blumenthal family. Monsieur and Madame Robert Blumenthal engaged her as governess for their two children, Marcel and Monique. They were referred to as Monsieur and Madame Robert. The French frequently use first names as a form of address, and my parents were called Monsieur and Madame Henri. Madame Robert had a brother, Vladek, who married Marthe Spitzer, Maman's friend. Marthe, her sister Nadine, and their parents, Eveline and Isidore Spitzer, became Maman's protectors. At this time, a young woman was considered an old maid if not engaged or married by age eighteen. Eveline decided to find a *schidech* (match) for Maman, introduced my parents to each other, and subsequently organized the wedding. In the ceremonial photograph, my parents seem pensive: Mother in white, with lacy veil, and Father, wearing a black tuxedo, hairline already receding. They were holding each other closely. I often wondered if they were happy in this arranged marriage. During the first six years of my life, my parents lavished all the love and attention not shared with one another on me. They certainly were different: Papa, quiet and introspective, Maman, a lively little bundle of nerves. Their arguments revealed their temperaments. Maman would bellow her complaints and displeasure interspersed with flowery curses, wildly gesticulating, plump arms moving in all directions, while Papa, calmly continued reading the newspaper and smoking a cigarette, sitting with a schnapps in hand, seemingly unperturbed. When the sound reached a certain crescendo, he would just calmly rise, take a hat and overcoat, and leave the house; perhaps to walk, or sit at a café to relieve the tension. I observed these scenes with dread, always wondering if Papa would return. He always did, and I felt secure again.

When Maman became the wife of the *patron* or boss of a factory, the self-conscious immigrant acquired more self-assurance. The newfound status and appearance assumed a great importance for her. Tiny and buxom, Maman never reached more than five feet in height, despite four-inch heels, or when taking a deep breath! Her hair, which was very fine and dark, did not please her and therefore, was dyed auburn. To add pizzazz and body, hours were spent attaching a thick hairpiece of similar color and consistency. Maman plucked her eyebrows to a thin line, emulating the movie stars of the period. Her face, already very pale in the morning, was powdered and rouged later in the day. Bright red lipstick was applied without a mirror (*this feat was so admired that I still emulate it today!*). She had a tiny upturned nose which was envied since mine is slightly crooked due to a childhood fall. An apparent florid complexion did not truly reflect Maman's health status, since she had undergone a kidney operation soon after pregnancy and developed hypertension lasting the remainder of her life. Maman loved flamboyant clothing, which she thought elegant when in fact the colors of the various ensembles clashed brilliantly. Jewelry, especially eighteen-carat gold bracelets and huge diamonds rings, adorned her wrists and fingers. There were skunk and Persian fur coats in the closet (a mink would have followed, if not for the war). The young daughter of the *patron* owned a brown rabbit coat, and later, a gray fox. Madame Henri was a *nouveau riche*, but Maman never so viewed herself.

My mother enjoyed smoking cigarettes, in keeping with a new image and to rebel against Papa who also smoked but did not think it seemly for a lady. She would puff on a cigarette without inhaling, holding it on the side of the mouth in an affected manner, to imitate an actress or Madame Robert, the epitome of the *grande dame* in her eyes. However, there was no smoking on Saturdays in honor of *Shabbat* or on *Yom Kippur*. In keeping with her own religious perspective, she was convinced that ham was not pork because it was tasty.

Extremely superstitious, Maman spat three times "Tsoy!Tsoy!Tsoy!" to avoid the evil eye, "Keyn einehorre!" when something complimentary was said concerning me or my father. Similarly, we had to sit unmoving for five minutes before leaving on a long trip. In addition, it was required to bite into a piece of material when a button was sewn on my dress while wearing it, otherwise my intellect would be in jeopardy. These erstwhile voodoo rituals were invariably carried out under strong verbal protest and sarcastic snickering.

Maman played the *grande dame* in public well but, in private, would curse like a sailor, in Yiddish, Polish, or Russian, whichever came spontaneously to mind. Maman eventually learned some choice French curses which were quickly dropped as soon as I repeated them, and reverted to a favorite in Russian, I discovered later, dealing with "copulating with your mother!!" The harsh tone of voice in these circumstances made me extremely nervous. This anxiety manifested itself by fear of sleeping alone in the dark and flagrant nail-chewing. The latter once caused Maman to pursue me in the kitchen, with a sharp knife used to prepare supper, shouting, "Ich werd dir arroysnehmen die kishkes!" (I'll take out your entrails!) Threats in Yiddish sound horrendous, but I was accustomed to them and understood that this was just an act. I recall goading her, by running around the table. She finally would give up. Such scenes helped precipitate the despicable habit with more relish than ever. Every Saturday,

Maman would inspect my nails with a frowning face. I knew what was coming because my cuticles were bleeding and my nails were bitten almost to the bone, for which I received a *frask* (a slap on the face) or a *setz* (a blow on the side). Cajoling and threats did not help. It was a nightmare for both of us. Then, as a proper example for me to emulate, she would extend her fingers with bright red nails. "Du sehst?" (You see?) glaring at me. I was not impressed. Week after week the conflict repeated itself. It never occurred to my parents to discover what problems provoked my behavior. Then, psychological help appeared chiefly directed for the deeply neurotic or the outright insane and was considered inappropriate, just for a nail-biting, upper-middle-class French Jewish girl.

Maman was obsessed with my health. How often have I heard the story of my intestinal operation? I was nine months old and apparently, nearly died. She never forgave the surgeon, a *nichtgitnik* (a good for nothing), and the wonderful nuns, *sollen zey zine gezind* (they should be well), of Saint Antoine Hospital. Later, she particularly resented the doctor who removed my tonsils. Quite a traumatic experience! Imagine a screaming child in a straight jacket, with mouth pried and kept open by metallic forceps, anesthetized while sitting on the lap of a buxom nurse and awakening with severe sore throat. The doctor had prescribed Methylene Blue application to ease the pain. The unpleasantness was soon forgotten on contemplating the soothing ice cream that Papa brought to console me.

After these memorable experiences, especially after contracting most of the "children's" diseases, Maman observed me closely and often complained to Papa that I did not eat enough. All food on the plate had to be swallowed because poor children in Russia were suffering of hunger (*so, send it to them!*).

Pallor indicated poor blood for which there were two dreaded solutions. A tablespoon of cod liver oil with breakfast would slither down my throat, followed by profuse crying and gagging. The second solution was not better. A *boucherie chevaline* (horse-meat butcher) was present in every district of Paris, with the model of a horse head mounted above the shop. Horse meat was supposedly most healthy.

To revitalize my blood, Maman tried to force me to eat those dreadful, rare, juicy steaks. I fought her all the way!

"Du muss dus essen" (you have to eat it), she yelled.

"Je n'aime pas le sang" (I don't like the blood), I yelled back.

"Blut west dir machen gesund und stark!" (Blood will make you healthy and strong!)

"Je n'veux pas!" (I don't wanna!) The idea that part of a horse could be eaten revolted me, having read Madame de Ségur's memoirs of a donkey who could think and feel. The horses seemed to be in the same family. Why hurt these poor animals? She finally gave up and ate the steaks herself.

**My grandmother Fanny**

**with Maman**

It was believed in France (now clinically confirmed) that a glass of wine (or more) a day is good for the arteries. Papa preferred a schnapps, but I was allowed a small quantity well diluted with water, the amount of which diminishing as I grew older. Good food is enhanced by wine, and enjoyed in moderation. Excess drinking, on the other hand, results in alcoholism, and *maladies du foie* (liver diseases) which according to the French, may or may not be cured at Vichy's waterspa! In true Gallic fashion, I grew up savouring wine and camembert cheese *bien fait* (ripe or runs in the middle).

Maman wanted me to be an accomplished young woman and have all the advantages she lacked as a child. Besides, to be completely assimilated in France, a young girl *de bonne famille* (of a good family), in addition to good manners, should also play the piano. Papa bought the instrument, an upright mahogany. On my sixth birthday, Madame Tryvous became my piano teacher. Madame was a Russian refugee, a large woman with heavy breasts and hips, who was delighted to speak Russian with my mother. Madame Tryvous addressed Maman as Vera Alexandrovna (the daughter of Alexander). It was as elegant as the *particule de*, sign of the French aristocracy. *Why couldn't I have a name like that?*

In cold weather, Maman, wanting to warm her before the lesson, would offer Madame Tryvous a glass of *tchai* (tea) and some cake while I dutifully listened to their incomprehensible conversation. They would sit and avidly gossip, their hands waving this way and that, interrupting only to pick up a cube of sugar, dunk it in the glass of tea, crunch it while sipping à la Russe, and munching on a piece of cake. I subsequently discovered that Madame Tryvous was very poor. She came regularly, but I usually was unprepared for the music assignments. This was another issue which provoked my mother who never gave up, however.

My personal appearance was just as important. Childhood photographs reveal a freckled little round face surrounded by curly black hair looking like a messy bird's nest. It was painful when Maman disentangled, combed, and tried to bind it together with a stiff and huge ribbon larger than my face. Although Shirley Temple's sausage curls were in vogue at the time, and I would have liked them, Maman preferred the bow.

One day, Madame Tryvous noticed me straining to decipher the notes. Of course, Maman promptly brought me to an ophthalmologist who prescribed glasses for nearsightedness, which I detested. Despite the corrective lenses, I sat in the first row in school. The large ribbon obstructed the view of my classmates, who vigorously protested. I had ambivalent feelings about it because the bow was also envied by the other girls. It made me look different and elegant, and one of my classmates, whose name was also Fernande, asked Maman to place a similar contraption on her hair. I was *mignonne* (cute), a little sprite with a winning smile, wearing a Shirley Temple dress, with flounces, gathered at the waist by a smooth silk sash. It had been sewn by Maman, as if made for a ball.

Maman was always there to comfort me. One of my favorite memories is being held by her when I was ill. Shalimar, a favorite perfume (now, my own), was reassuring. Maman was tiny and plump, and when seated, her feet did not quite reach the floor. I would climb up on her lap, slip down, and then climb up again. Maman would enfold me in her arms, a smile on her face, murmuring softly in a sweet and soothing voice, singing lullabies in Yiddish and Russian. When I occasionally hear them sung nowadays, the lyrics come to mind, and her image as well.

When I was nasty, she would say, "Venn ich bin nit mehr, vest du villen mir sehen durch a speltele" (When I'll be gone, you'll want to see me through a crack in the wall). It is so true. I began to understand my mother better while raising my own children. I was going to be "The Perfect Mom." My mother's mistakes would not be repeated.

I proceeded to make my own.

Maman, I wanted to be so different from you, yet these melodramatic scenarios repeat themselves. My children's reaction is reminiscent; a dismissive shrug of the shoulders! Sometimes one of them will pretend to play a sad tune on a make-believe violin!

A *Yiddishe Momme*, all over again!

# CHAPTER IV

## FAMILY LIFE IN PARIS—1930s

On the deck of our house, near the end of Long Island, overlooking the rippling waters of the creek, a family of swans glides peacefully by. It is so quiet, the only perceptible sound coming from the soft, windblown leaves in the trees. I cannot help contrasting my beautiful surroundings with the Paris neighborhood of my childhood.

Sometimes Maman would talk of the early years in her marriage, when there was little money available. She and my father were confined temporarily to a tiny room in Rue St. Maur, a working-class neighborhood.

"Why did you leave?" I asked.

"The rented apartment came with furniture including a flea-ridden mattress. It was disgusting, and we wanted to leave immediately but had nowhere else to go. Another place had to be found which turned out to be a flat in the Rue Tesson."

We remained in this lodging despite the poor neighborhood and Papa's financial success. It was easily accessible to the factory and relatively inexpensive as this period was economically and politically unstable. This street, at the junction of Rue St. Maur, is the one remembered and revisited after the war. A wine merchant and *bazar* (discount store) at the union of these streets had been replaced now by other establishments.

There was no elevator in the six-story dwelling. Small windows on each level permitted some light in the somber hallway. The *minuterie* had to be pressed to turn on the hall light which would last only one minute (to save electricity) before it had to be pressed again. Residents had to rush up the stairs in order not to be caught in the dark before reaching their respective doorways. Wanting to see the old quarters again and overcoming my reticence, I knocked on the door. It was opened by a smiling woman. Taking courage in hand, explaining the circumstances, I asked if I might look at the apartment and was invited in. Memories came rushing back.

There was the same dim corridor, which I ran through as a child. The rooms were arranged (in length) similar to a railroad car. The kitchen was located to the left of the hallway. Next came the room which was to have been mine. This did not happen because Maman (who would never win the *Better Homes and Gardens* Best Housekeeper Award) used it as an untidy storage area. Besides, frightened of the dark, I ended up sleeping in my parents' room, in a large crib. The well-lit dining room was at the end of the corridor. Queries from the lady of the house concerning my parents received vague responses, as I concentrated on the surroundings. Furniture was still sparse, the walls remained bare. The floor was now covered with tattered rugs, but I remember my mother's parquet floors which she periodically and lovingly polished with a piece of felt, on her hands and knees. It was her great pride, upon which we carefully shuffled, wearing *patins* (heavy fabric slippers) . . .

"Ah! Vous avez le chauffage central!" I exclaimed.

"Eh! Oui!" Then, there was no central heating. Instead, a wide black coal-burning stove stood in a corner. It was the only source of heat. Coal was obtained from the cellar, a dim place where one reluctantly ventured alone. The fireplace was never lit since Maman once observed the local chimney sweep covered with soot, coughing up blood, and feeling pity, was unwilling to let him clean it.

Slowly walking through these rooms, the night of Uncle Isaac's arrest flashed to mind, with its unpleasant memories. Leaning out the window to observe the street life was a favorite pastime as a child. A drunk would sometimes come by singing a French ditty, and Maman would give me some coins wrapped in newspaper to throw through the window, which occasionally would scatter over the street upon striking the ground. He would collect the money, yell "Merci," and continue the tune. Men shouting *chiffonnier* (rag picker), *charbonnier* (coal merchant), or *marchand de glace* (ice merchant) touted their wares. Mother, as ever protective, with the inevitable yell, would draw me safely back from the balustrade.

Having no friends, I would play alone in the dining room with a crate full of toys, mostly made from wooden heels from Papa's shoe factory. Maman continually sought the utensils which regularly disappeared from the kitchen drawer. Forks and spoons decorated with scraps of cotton became princes and princesses. My *nobles* were given aristocratic names using the *particule de* found in my favorite tales.

In the adjacent room, Maman fashioned my dresses on the sewing machine, hands maneuvering the fabric, feet pedaling away, singing along with Danielle Darrieux's rendition of: "ça fait boum, là dans mon coeur," or Charles Trenet's "Y'a d'la joie," on the radio. Periodically a piece of fruit or other goody was brought in; simply an excuse to peek in on me.

Toys and books were sufficient to keep me occupied. Many hours were spent in the WC (water-closet or lavatory), escaping Maman's interference, where a rampant imagination created a fantasy kingdom with me as queen. My train of thought was usually interrupted by Maman, who, by now exasperated, demanded that my *mysses* (stories) be completed!

When I was six years old, dressed to the nines in a new outfit, and tightly clutching Maman's hand, I was accompanied to first day in kindergarten. The school looked as forbidding as a prison, high stone walls enclosing a yard with a few scraggly trees. Two young teachers welcomed us. One crouched near me with a reassuring smile, took my hand, describing the day in school, and stood up, saying, "Au-revoir Maman! A bientôt!" I turned toward my mother, ready to shout, "Please, don't leave me," but then, I noticed boys and girls running around the yard, laughing. They seemed to be enjoying themselves, and so could I! Instead of weeping, I cheerfully waved goodbye. From this day on, I was impatient to go to school.

Discipline was strict in class. Everyone arose when the principal or instructor entered. Silence was mandatory. Should it be broken by only one nonconfessing culprit, the entire class was punished; hands crossed on the desk, eyes straight ahead; no sound was heard for ten minutes. The discovered offender had to face the wall, wearing a dunce hat. This atmosphere did not upset me; school had opened a new world, so different from the familiar one at home. An attentive student, I quickly learned reading and writing. I looked forward to the day when Papa would no longer have to read to me.

After school, if there was not much homework, Maman and I went to Papa's factory on the Avenue Parmentier, which was a special treat. Then, it seemed a long distance to walk for a little girl. Maman either had to carry me, or allow me to rest. Passing the *pâtisserie*, the tempting display and aromas of *petits fours, éclairs, babas au rhum, mille-feuilles* lured us in. Maman bought a *Pain au chocolat*, which I munched with relish. Occasionally, at the street corner, an entertainer would sing a popular ditty accompanied by a small band of musicians including an accordionist. At its conclusion, a musician's hat was passed to the audience for contributions, while efforts were made to sell the sheet music of the tune.

At the factory, Papa was always pleased to see us. Max, his partner, seemed pompous and angry, reminding me in later years of Mussolini. Then a feeling of antipathy pervaded my greetings to him, which were polite but curt. While Maman would gossip with Max and one of the secretaries, Papa sometimes took me for a tour of the factory, talking with the workers, assuring that the shoes were properly manufactured. Invariably, I returned home with a new pair, after an adventurous trip in the métro (subway). What fun it was to have your ticket punched by the *poinçonneur,* and how exciting to squeeze through the automatic gate before it closed on the train's arrival! Maman, understandably, did not release my hand, as we silently stood on the platform, waiting for the next train. Sitting in the subway car as it sped away, I was hypnotized by the passing, repetitive wine ad: "Dubo, Dubon, Dubonnet," plastered to the lighted métro tunnel wall and extended from one station to another.

The open market in the *quartier* (quarter) was held several times a week. The farmers brought their products from the country, which were spread beneath tents in adjacent stalls. Intrigued, I followed Maman, as she carefully chose fresh vegetables, fruit, or whole fish which were displayed on ice and green leaves. The best array and enticing aromas came from the *crèmerie* with its hundred varieties of cheese and blocks of butter. Maman never left this particular stall without a chunk of the latter, cut with a guillotine-type slicer, a camembert *bien fait*, and a soft white cheese called *Petit Suisse* which apparently had miraculous, beneficial effects on children's growth. The meat department was ignored because it was not *Kasher*. I was just as glad, as the eyes of skinned rabbits hanging from the tents' rafters seem to follow us.

My favorite grand excitement was food shopping in Belleville, in the east end of Paris. Belleville and the *Pletzl* in the Marais district were the two principal Jewish quarters. Belleville remains a poor district, but the *Pletzl* now has a certain cachet. The Marais, with its sixteenth—and seventeenth-century-old mansions, has been renovated and is much in fashion.

Then, the appetizing smell (should you happen to like it) of cooking chicken fat (*schmaltz*), onions, and garlic pervaded the narrow streets, while in stark contrast, unpleasant odors emanated from the *Vespasiennes* or *Pissoirs*. I would hop on the uneven cobblestones, trying to maintain my balance, and wondered how policemen wearing heavy navy capes could maneuver bicycles, so skillfully, on these streets without falling.

Yiddish appeared to be the only language spoken. Maman was in her element, savoring the visit to each of the various shops, stopping here for pickles, there for marinated herring, and finally at the butcher's, who came from the same *shtetl*. The gossip would have gone on endlessly (Maman was very talkative), had I not impatiently nudged her. She would then end the conversation by discussing the quality and price of the meat, which was expected. Leave would at last be taken after much embracing and kissing.

Papa's sister, Aunt Régine, who came from Warsaw to live in Belleville, had married a Polish-Jewish émigré, Paul Schmelniecki. Thérèse, his daughter from a previous marriage, hated her stepmother. Tata Régine adored her son François, who was my age, and detested Thérèse, three years my senior. At the time, the age difference was significant. Thérèse and I scarcely communicated. Tata Régine neither resembled my father physically, nor had his mild temperament. She was a tall and skinny woman, with dark hair and eyes that remind me of "The Wicked Witch of the West" from *The Wizard of Oz*. Maman had some vociferous arguments with her. François and I were named after our paternal grandfather, and both wore eyeglasses. Those were the only shared characteristics. On those rare occasions when our mothers were on speaking terms, the Belleville shopping tour would often conclude in Tata Régine's apartment for a *glasele tchai un' kichel* (a little glass of tea and cake). Inspired by the current events, combat was my cousin François' favorite game, with me as the designated evil German, and he, the brave Frenchman! Armed with toy guns, we engaged in make-believe battles, running around the apartment with wild shouts, and had such a wonderful time that Maman had to literally drag me home, despite my protests and tears, only after assurances of an early return visit.

Some Saturday evenings, Papa, Maman, and I went to visit Tata Eveline, near the *République* quarter. Marthe and Nadine, her daughters, played current popular tunes for the piano without sheet music. On cold winter nights my father, Tonton Isidore, and Vladek, Marthe's husband, played belote. This French cardgame, much like pinochle, was lively; the men raucous. Tata

Eveline prepared *tchai* in the *samovar* (elaborate, old-fashioned Russian tea maker), and cakes in the kitchen, while chattering with Maman. I felt protected and warm, watching Nadine stoking the fire in the coal-burning stove, while Marthe fed her baby, her opulent breasts bare for all to see. Intrigued, I would look with speculative interest while Vladek, her husband, would leave the card game momentarily to give her a passionate kiss, often touching his crotch at the same time.

"Maman, pourquoi Vladek, il se gratte là, entre ses jambes?" (Why is Vladek scratching himself down there, between his legs?) I asked, puzzled, one day.

"Nu, er kratzt sech" (So, he is scratching himself).

"Marthe is glicklich" (Marthe is lucky), Maman continued with a smirk, "zu hobben a man wus hot ihr azey lieb" (to have a man who loves her so).

Of course, this implied that Papa did not "love" Maman.

The question of the sisters' "reputation" was invariably raised. "Nadine is a *coorve*, *du vehst*" (Nadine is a *coorve*, you know), she declared to Papa, who was vaguely listening. My curiosity was piqued.

"Maman, qu'est-ce que c'est a *coorve*?" (Maman, what is a *coorve*?)

"Shah, shtill, du darfst nit vissen!" (Keep quiet, it's not for you to know!)

"Pourquoi j' peux pas savoir, Maman, dis-moi c' que c'est?" (Why can't I know, Maman? Please tell me what it is.)

"C'est ine poule." (*A chicken? I thought.*) Perplexed, I kept quiet, having received a simple answer which did not make any sense, and much later discovering that the words *coorve* and *poule* meant "slut." Nadine liked men and was reputed to have many lovers until she married. Maman's animosity was then not readily comprehensible, but now, I assume that perhaps jealousy of the two pretty sisters (whom I personally liked) was the cause. The women singing, accompanied by Marthe at the piano, were the highlights of the evening. Their repertoire included: "Ot a yid a veibbele" (A Jew Has Such a Wife!), "Rozhinkes mit mandlen"

(Raisins and Almonds Lullaby), "In Odess" (In Odessa) or "otchi tchornya" (Dark Eyes) in Yiddish and Russian.

Enthralled by the music, I twirled and whirled around the room and, finally, exhausted, collapsed against Maman, who took me in the adjacent room to rest on the sofa. A large white bear skin warmed the floor. Initially, the beast's frightening glare prevented my falling asleep. Maman sat nearby and sang reassuringly. Later, Bear Skin became my friend, with its open huge mouth and sharp teeth. At least it seemed friendly . . . it did not move. Looking at its expressionless eyes, I felt hypnotized. Lulled by the noisy laughter and conversation spilling from next door, my eyes closed. Sometime in the early-morning hours, Maman awakened me for the trip home.

As a true Frenchman, Papa reserved Sundays for the family and enjoyed having his nieces close by. Tata Fanny had two sisters, Suzanne and Jeannette. Old photographs of Tata Fanny reveal her resemblance to Papa: the same square face, but with beautiful almond-shaped dark eyes magnified by eyeglasses! She was my favorite. Tata Jeannette, who almost always had a smile, was likable, in contrast to Tata Suzanne who appeared withdrawn, sly, and had a persistent smirk.

Some Sundays, they would visit our apartment. Lunch, including dessert and tea, was interminable. Seated at the table throughout the day, and usually without intermission, the festivities concluded with a multicourse dinner. The premier event occurred when Jeannette's husband, Jean, was coaxed (without much difficulty) into singing, "sur la pointe des pieds!" (on the tip of your toes!), after a few glasses of wine. This was accomplished off-key, with much gusto, and slightly slurred speech; the audience heartily laughing, while Florette and I snickered and grimaced.

Passover was a yearly, joyful occasion reuniting the family. Florette and I had no concept of what it represented, only that *Pesach* meant favorite Jewish foods would be *à table*. Only in later years did I learn to appreciate typical French cuisine. Papa liked oysters and mussels, and so did I. Frogs' legs, escargots were delicacies unknown to me (still are). Pork (except for ham, my mother's indulgence) was taboo at home. It still is. However, barbecued pork spareribs (well done) in a Chinese restaurant, even today, remain an important exception. At Passover, Maman shopped for days and cooked long hours to make this celebration something special, by preparing a wonderful meal. A live carp had been kept in the bathtub for several days, to ensure freshness. Obviously, nobody could bathe during this period. On the other hand, daily baths were most unusual in France, anyway in those days. I still recall with horror as tiny Maman raised the ax to guillotine the poor bucking carp on the kitchen table. She was fierce. Of course, the "gefilte fish," which resulted from this execution, was delicious. The carp was cut in slices, finely chopped, mixed with eggs, matzo meal, onions, and spices, made into individual patties which were surrounded by portions of fish skin, and cooked, then placed in a circular fashion, about the periphery of a large plate, and garnished with sliced carrots. The head of the carp preened in its place of honor in the center of the dish, with a piece of carrot in its mouth. The traditional chicken was plucked and cleaned, its head having suffered the same fate as the carp's. *Kreplach*, Jewish raviolis, an Eastern European delicacy, were filled with finely chopped beef. Her recipe for *kneidlach*, matzomeal dumplings, was as light as could be. That was a feat in itself since *kneidlach*, if improperly made, can feel heavy as lead and cause a variety of digestive ills, not the least of which are persistent bloating and gas. The stuffed derma (intestines), *tsimmes* (stewed carrots and prunes), roast chicken, and beef *flanken* were succulent. Exclamations of delight greeted each dish. These long hours of preparation for Passover were spent in the kitchen with Maman dressed to kill, auburn hair in a pompadour and fingernails blood-red.

For the newly initiated, the greatest delicacies were the carp's head and the chicken's feet. Maman seriously concentrated on sucking the marrow of every bone. I declined this queasy endeavor. My favorite was her cake, a scrumptious concoction of flour, eggs, and butter . . . which of course was not kosher for Passover, but who cared? Certainly not our crowd. The family arrived. Exchange of kisses was *de rigueur*: two, three, sometimes four and with great affection. Exceptionally, Tata Suzanne would only lightly brush a cheek. Men did not escape the ritual: shaking hands was for strangers. Then, an apéritif was served: Pernod, or red Vermouth, without hors d'oeuvre. Maman wanted everyone hungry, and we were.

Only many years later, after immigrating to the United States, did I learn of the significance of Passover (as well as the other Jewish holidays). Then, there were no *Haggadahs* relating the story of Moses and the Israelites' Exodus from bondage in Egypt, just good food, wine, a merry time, and Tonton Jean's *"Sur la pointe des pieds!"* If anyone was still sober, Papa would organize a game of belote with the men, while the women washed dishes and discussed current events. The children circulated within the apartment, singing, fighting, and laughing.

A family occasion which remains well engraved in memory is the *Briss* (circumcision) of little baby boy Michel, the son of Tata Suzanne and Tonton Emile, her husband. Friends and family were gathered around the baby and the rabbi, laughing noisily. Tata Suzanne looked nervous and sobbed. Florette, François, and I were in constant motion, giggling and obnoxiously trying to push ourselves through the male barrier, which prevented us from observing the ceremony. The men protested. The shoving stopped. The children were taken to another room; the door firmly closed, with a stern warning not to exit until permission was granted, or else . . . Nevertheless, the baby's screaming, the women's weeping, and the men's praying could be heard through the door. The noise was terrifying. What was going on? No longer anxious to see the "happening," we went about playing our own games. Many years later, the second *Briss* that I refused to watch was that of my son Marc-David, but I subsequently became somewhat more courageous for those of my grandsons, Arieh and Daniel, but still not sufficiently, to observe the ritual directly.

My early childhood was a happy one, revolving around a loving family and school, insulated from world events. It was tranquil, focused, and protected. Subsequent, shattering events changed it all, and I was never the same again.

# CHAPTER V

## PREWAR UNREST

Historically, France has undergone frequent periods of political turmoil. (9) The first inkling of Post-World War I unrest in France occurred in 1936 during the *Front Populaire* (Popular Front) which was created in 1934 in strong opposition to fascism. The objectives of its program were the dissolution of right-wing organizations, defense of public schools, trade unions' rights, diminish unemployment, introduction of the forty-hour working week, *Congés payés* or paid vacation, and development of public works. (10) Léon Blum, the prime minister, worked to introduce these socialistic reforms. Blum, a Jew, faced the anti-Semitism prevalent in France and had many political enemies. The French were also politically divided as concerns the Spanish Civil War for the communists favored the Loyalists Republicans. The Royalists were for Franco's fascists, and people volunteered to fight on each side. This civil strife occurred in Paris during the period of 1934–1937. (11)

On February 6, 1934, at the Place de la Concorde, demonstrators of the extreme-right attempted to invade the *Chambre des Deputés* (National Assembly), shouting, "A bas les voleurs" (down with the thieves), and hoping that the *Croix de Feu* World War I veteran's organization would help them. The *Croix de Feu* did not respond, and the mounted *Garde Républicaine*, saber in hand, dispersed the demonstrators. (12)

This demonstration by the Right was a violent reaction in support of the Spanish fascists and against the Bolsheviks, thought to be more dangerous than the *Boches*. A few days later, a counter manifestation by the Left brought forth the Popular Front. The extreme right believed that Hitler was better than Blum. The workers, however, never forgot the *congés payés*, for which he may have received a singular thank you, after the war. (13)

Demonstrations continued periodically during these years. One such incident vividly comes to mind, although I was only five years of age at the time. That particular evening, Papa is late for dinner. Maman sets the table, worriedly listening to the radio. The announcer speaks about the mayhem in the streets of Paris. Maman's anxiety is transmitted to me, although I do not fully understand what is being said. There is no way to determine why Papa is delayed. A telephone is a luxury my parents cannot afford. Friends and family are distant. Finally the sound of a key is heard. He is home. Usually, as the door opens in the evenings, I joyfully jump in his arms, not allowing him time to remove his topcoat and hat. Papa always dresses well and neatly, in custom-made, conservative suits and matching ties. This time, he is unsmiling, disheveled, and quite excited. There was a narrow escape at the Place de la République. Parisian workers were protesting in support of the *Front Populaire* and literally tearing up the street pavement to build barricades. (14) Dinner that night is spent discussing these events, the resulting rumors, and also the current unrest in Germany. Observing Father's frowns and worried look upset me too, given my close attachment.

The shoe factory was successful in spite of these events. A new pair of shoes or sandals accompanied each outfit that Maman created for me. After the Depression in Germany and France, there was a prevalent distrust of banks, especially savings institutions. Therefore, Papa bought dollars and gold, the latter in old French coins as "Louis." Maman also was bedecked in diamond rings and gold jewelry. Birthday gifts consisted chiefly of books and jewelry. I preferred the former but still possess a gold bracelet and necklace received at the time. Papa hid these valuables in "a safe" built in the bedroom wall, usually accomplished while I was in school. It was well camouflaged by a block of plaster covered with wallpaper; once seeing Maman near the *cachette*, I somehow instinctively understood but never referred to it.

Generally, my parents blissfully ignored the current unpleasant news. On the other hand, the visit of King George VI and Queen Elizabeth of England in July 1938 to France was a great occasion for my mother, having once dreamed of receiving an invitation to the coronation. Maman had closely followed the scandal involving Edward VIII and Mrs. Simpson with special interest, and while very angry at the king for abdicating, at the same time, empathized with this tale of "true love." Devouring the newspapers stories, especially in *Paris-Soir* (a popular tabloid), Maman shared the dilemma of Madame Lebrun, the French president's wife who was unable to decide whether to make reverence to the queen or not! Maman constantly discussed this event when the family visited. Papa would roll his eyes with a smirk on his face and sip his schnapps.

Anti-Semitism was flourishing in France, and my father ignored it. Right-wing newspapers *Gringoire* and *Je Suis Partout* expressed the anger of the fascists who blamed the economic difficulties of France on the Jews and were opposed to the immigration and naturalization laws to help the thousands of Jews fleeing Germany, Austria, and Czechoslovakia. Newspaper articles declared that the Jews had communist tendencies and dominated the professions (*familiar refrain*). Many areas were tainted. The cities in which this propaganda flourished included Paris, of course, but also Strasbourg, Lyon, and Orléans where it was said that all the officials were Jews. (15) The political Right approved of Neville Chamberlain, the prime minister of England, whose efforts were considered a diplomatic success at Munich in September of 1938. It was said that nonintervention meant nonescalation of the war fever with Germany, and that there was too much hysteria about so-called fascism. The Munich Accord appeased the Nazis by dividing Czechoslovakia and giving them the Sudetenland. Strangely, Papa, among many others, also thought that Chamberlain had been successful and that the Germans would be satisfied. However, Munich only seemed to whet Hitler's appetite for more territory. (16) Papa recalled that Chamberlain and his umbrella were mocked and despised when Hitler occupied all of Czechoslovakia shortly thereafter! Then his name was phonetically pronounced *J'aime Berlin* (I love Berlin). What irony!

In December 1938, Papa's cousins came to Paris on their way to the United States. Henry Hertstein, his wife Betty, and their son Frankie had left Berlin, the city of their birth and residence as German citizens. Papa had first made their acquaintance while in Berlin. They remained with us for a few days. I was curious to know why their name was Hertstein and not Horensztajn. Apparently, Jews from the same family, in the Diaspora, frequently changed their names or spelling thereof. (There were also relatives whose name was Gerstein.) Henry and Betty told of frightening events in Germany, confirming the rumors which included the burning of books written by Jews and other "undesirables" (in the streets of Berlin in 1933), restriction of Jews in the professions and schools, and terror attacks carried out on November 9 and 10, 1938, in Germany and Austria against hundreds of synagogues and Jewish-owned stores. This came to be known as *Kristallnacht* or "Night of the Broken Glass" and was Hitler's revenge for the assassination of a German diplomat, Ernst von Rath, by a young Jewish man in Paris, Herschel Grynspan, whose parents had died in a concentration camp.

The Hertsteins had left with few belongings and valuables to help them start anew in the United States. They begged my parents to join them, predicting the events in Germany would be repeated in France.

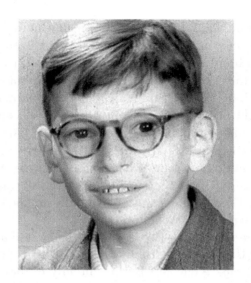

My cousin François

Sables d'Olonne, in the late 1930s
With my cousin Florette

**My cousin Fanny, her daughter Florette and son Marc**

Papa smilingly replied, "I left Poland to escape pogroms and remained in Germany for eight years. As you know I never liked the Germans. That's why I came to France and made a good life for myself and family here. What will I do in America?"

"The same as you do here," responded Henry without any hesitation.

"These terrible things could never happen in France. The French are not like that!" Papa affirmed.

"That's what we said in Germany too!" Henry insisted. To no avail. Later, Papa remembered this conversation on many occasions and regretted not following their advice.

Life continued, as if everything was perfectly normal. The New Year 1939 was celebrated with a party at a Parisian restaurant. Tata Fanny, her husband Georges, and cousin Florette had joined us. Baby boy Marc was at home with his grandmother. Dressed in our finest, heedless of the situation or perhaps because of it, the family strove to enjoy the evening. Florette continuously cast frightened glances at her father after being reprimanded in a sharp tone of voice accompanied by a withering look.

"What's the matter?" I murmured to my cousin.

"I almost did not come tonight because I did not respond fast enough with the multiplication tables. I am scared of him." The poor girl was trying not to cry. I squeezed her hand, and we smiled at each other like conspirators. There was wonderful food aplenty; wine and champagne flowed for the adults. Leaving the restaurant, Papa and Tonton Georges, exceptionally happy, with arms entwined, loudly sang Maurice Chevalier's popular tunes of the day, while the wives laughed indulgently. We followed, bewildered by the adults' behavior. I had never seen Papa lose control before.

Parisians were celebrating in the streets. Despite the historical conflicts between France and Germany, they thought that another war defied logic. This was the calm before the tempest. Perhaps people wished to suppress their subconscious fears (at least temporarily).

Summers were spent at the Sables d'Olonne in the Vendée, along the Atlantic coast; Papa could only take a week's vacation or two due to his responsibilities at the shoe factory. The beach is wide, the sand white and clean. In the morning, at low tide, mounted riders galloped their horses. Florette and I, age seven, dreaded the long walk to the ocean which appeared so distant and seemed to take forever. Once in the water, however, it was great fun, playing tag with the breakers. The Promenade, a high grayish white cliff overlooking the sea, broke the waves, which at high tide came crashing against it. Small houses lined the Promenade, and in the evenings, friends, lovers, and families took "a walk" or sat at the terraces of the cafés, observing passersby, listening to the soothing sound of the ocean and the accordion music filtering through from neighboring cafés. It was a good life.

On returning to Sables d'Olonne after the war, the beach was still our domain during the day, replaced by cafés on the Promenade in the evening. Courageous young men approached our table, under the intense scrutiny of our parent chaperons (since Florette and I were teenagers), inviting us to the dance floor. Usually, we danced together, coaching each other in the rumba or the boogie-woogie, laughingly competing for the lead.

The summer in 1939 was awaited with great expectation: the trip on the train, sleeping in *a couchette*, sharing a picnic of cold chicken and baguettes with the family, while watching the landscapes fly by. Aunt Suzanne also came with baby Michel, as well as Aunt Jeannette and her daughters, Francine, who was Marc's age, and baby Lucette. At night, the train's monotonous sounds of engine and wheels lulled us to sleep. I never slept better. The pungent smell of fish greeted us on arrival . . .

Sables d'Olonne is a port and fresh seafood, the staple of the community. A small rented house was shared with all the relatives, but the beach was really our home during the long day. Once in the sea, Maman and Tata Fanny had difficulty persuading Florette and me to leave it. However, observing other children playing in the sand induced us to follow suit. We built castles, played house, and baked sand cakes that were decorated with colored chalk. I envied Florette who was tanned after one day. My skin was very white and covered with many freckles. The first week of exposure to the sun's rays was always painful, resulting in blistering red (as a lobster) skin despite Maman's nightly applications of talcum powder. No sunblock in those days! At the end of the week, it was pleasurable to peel away. Late in the summer, my freckles had conjoined, appearing as uneven brown pigmentation.

Totally unaware of international events, and in addition to Florette's deepening tan, my greatest concern was her regional folklore costume. Walking on the Promenade, the *Sablaises* appeared elegant and graceful. The girls and women wore a short-pleated black skirt, lacy white blouse, and a colorful shawl crisscrossed across the bust, black silk stockings and wooden clogs, their color as vivid as the shawls, which made a pleasant, clacking sound as they walked. A high *coiffe* of white lace completed the outfit. Tata Fanny had bought this costume for Florette for an upcoming birthday, and my cousin delighted in parading about, thus attired, to my great frustration. Poor Maman became annoyed with my demands for similar dress, which were ignored; the outfit was expensive and unnecessary. That was that. A reluctant promise though was finally obtained after much pleading, "Maybe for my birthday, maybe! Please, Maman, pleeeeease!" Florette's was celebrated on September 2, 1939. On this occasion, even the children were permitted to drink wine with dinner, although theirs was well diluted with water. I recall going to bed a bit tipsy.

During the night, the voices of Papa and uncles Emile and Jean and Mother's crying awaken me. Frightened, I jump out of bed, hurry to the living room, and throw myself in Papa's arms. He presses me closely. "What's the matter?" I begin anxiously.

"Papa has to be a soldier and fight the Germans," replies my father, with a very solemn face.

"The French and the English have declared war on Germany, after the invasion of Poland by Hitler on September 1, and the government is mobilizing," says Tonton Jean.

Mother is sobbing, and I try to comfort her, arms encircling her neck, to no avail. I start to cry too. *Something terrible is going to happen to Papa. I know it. He is leaving and is going to die. I won't see him anymore.*

"This is going to be a short war, you will see," Papa affirms reassuringly, "the Maginot line will stop the Germans, and we shall win." My uncles Jean and Emile, who came with Papa to say goodbye to their families, reinforce this declaration with forceful nods of their heads. Indeed!

Papa's confidence and trust in the Maginot line, the "impregnable" defensive wall of France (17) are also mirrored in the faces of Tonton Jean and Emile.

However, his patriotism was not appreciated by the government. Two weeks later, Papa and Tonton Paul, Tata Régine's husband, returned. The authorities had refused their enlistment because they were not French citizens. Papa, who wanted to fight for France, was disappointed. Emile and Jean were French and went to the front. Uncle Georges, conspicuously absent at that time, kept on appearing and disappearing from the scene, finally abandoning his family. He suddenly showed up after the war. Nobody welcomed him.

Everyone was so optimistic; the war would end shortly with the French victorious, just as in 1918, forgetting that the First World War had lasted four years!

# CHAPTER VI

## PARIS, OPEN CITY

In 1870 and later in 1918, French civilians were directly exposed to war. By 1939, the unthinkable happens: the nation prepares for war again. Civil servants, soldiers, and police wearing identifying colored armbands are organized to direct and protect the population. Civilians are required to have a first-aid kit, water supply, and of course, a gas mask. The Germans had used poison gas in World War I, on the battlefield. Now the French prepare for the worst eventuality. The gas masks are taken everywhere. Initially, there is a specially designed minicar to detect poison gas, which would transmit a rhythmic, sharp sound in its presence. As a result many Parisians put on the masks unnecessarily, whenever a police car horn is heard. When it is finally realized that poison gas is not to be used by the Germans, the shape of the mask is memorialized as souvenir cast for bottles of brandy or perfume! (18)

Schoolchildren are also taught how to use these bizarre, rubbery-smelling contraptions with two enormous, transparent "eyes" and an extended curved tube resembling an elephant's trunk. Two teachers are needed to place this monstrosity over my face, as I am screaming and kicking, until ultimately, reluctantly submit. It is scary and difficult to breathe. As I am trying to control my nausea, and perspiring profusely, one of the instructors says soothingly, "N'aie pas peur! Laisse-toi aller!" (Don't be scared, let yourself go!) *She can't be serious! How can I relax while choking?* Nevertheless, the words have a calming effect. Nearby, other children are also rebelling, and the classroom becomes like a war zone. Some are more courageous than others. It requires a few practice sessions to gradually become accustomed to these "ugly devices," finally, able to laugh at our comical appearance. The teachers explain that civilians must be prepared to respond to sirens, particularly at night, warning the population to enter air-raid, available shelters (in basements or the métro).

Maman prepares a small suitcase with some bedding, and a first-aid kit. Every evening before going to bed, the suitcase and gas masks are placed near the apartment's entrance door. There are ninety-two siren locations in Paris. The initial warning is in the middle of the night. When the shrill sound of the first siren is about to cease, another commences, and so on, until all sirens have responded. The teachers have done their job well. I am prepared.

*Look Maman, Papa, what I can do?* strapping the gas mask in its container on my shoulder and skipping, skip, skip up and down to the métro. Paris is totally dark; sirens continue blaring ceaselessly. Small pocket lamps, tinted blue or orange, guide the civilians. Some people become anxious at the shrill sound of the sirens and run, while others walk calmly to the subway, which now serves as an air-raid shelter. We descend into a dark abyss. The noise is deafening, children are crying, men with armbands shout instructions and blow their whistles. Electrical power is cut off. Dim light is provided by hand-held lamps, but it is difficult to see. The platforms are already full of people who gradually climb down to the bare tracks. The sirens can no longer be heard. Papa helps Maman arrange a small area for us, with blankets and pillows. Families nearby do the same.

"Excusez-moi, Madame, si je vous dérange . . ." (Excuse me, Madame, I hope I don't disturb you . . .) A conversation has promptly started between our immediate neighbor and Maman.

"I hope the electricity remains off," remarks Maman to the

skinny woman and her portly husband, who are comfortably settling their little boy in a huge *édredon* (comforter). "We don't want to be electrocuted," Maman added.

"Vous avez raison (you are right). I hope so too," replies the woman, a worried look on her face. "Did you know," she continues, "that a terrible accident happened during the first alert, in September, when three women were seriously burnt because the current was mistakenly turned on?"

"Did they die?" an even more troubled Maman inquires.

"No! Thank God!" the woman states reassuringly then, as an afterthought, said, "have you closed the door of your apartment with the key?"

"Why?" Another worry materializes.

"Some homes have been burglarized!"

"Oh! Dear God! Henri, what are we going to do? Thieves are going to come to our house."

"Hack nicht a tchainik." (Don't say stupid things; literally: don't knock on the teapot.)

"Everything will be fine, you'll see, Vera!" My father, as always, looks on the bright side.

For me, "c'est la grande aventure."

Civilians cannot leave the métro until so permitted by the security staff, who is expected to know when it is safe but too often is no more knowledgeable than the civilians whom it is there to protect. It is like the blind leading the blind.

During the first alarm, I can't fall asleep, observing with curiosity the people around me who seem to take the event in stride, without panic, as if at an outing or picnic. This adventure becomes eventually routine, and sleep comes more easily. On returning safely home, Maman checks to ensure that the apartment is in order. Nothing has been stolen.

Every evening I lie in bed, in anticipation of another German air raid, which is now frequent. The family retires early to try to sleep before the nocturnal visit to the métro. Maman becomes overly optimistic one night, thinking that no raid will occur, and does not make the usual preparations. Blaring sirens interrupt our deep slumber and brings panic to the household. Maman, trying to find suitable clothing, throws them haphazardly out of the closet. Her hands tremble as she dresses me.

"Maman, Maman, I am wearing two different socks!" I exclaim, laughing. Silently grabbing my hand, she drags me out the apartment, dressing on the way and, as we rush down the subway stairs, suddenly realizes that Papa is not with us. *Where is he?* Maman wants to cry. Sensing her anxiety, my heart is beating fast. *Papa is dead. I am sure. We'll find his body torn by a bomb.* Maman stands for a minute undecided, eyes wild, searching the milling crowd, crushing my hand. We rush home . . . only to find the culprit gazing out the window without apparent concern, smoking a cigarette, having decided to stay and observe the bombing! A lonely candle lights eerily the room.

Torn between relief and anger, Maman yells. Papa responds in kind. Now I want to cry.

"Wos is mit dir? (What's the matter with you?) You know it is dangerous to stay home. You could have been killed!" screams my mother.

"But you see, nothing happened," answers Papa calmly.

"They say that the light of your cigarette at the window can attract the attention of the enemy!"

"Dus is narishkeiten! (What nonsense!) What's going to happen, will happen! What's the use in leaving!"

He then adds with a sigh: "There is no life in Paris anymore! The cinema closes at ten in the evening, and one has to be near a shelter in case of an air raid!"

Maman and Papa are fighting again. This time though, silently, I agree with my mother. *Why did he do that? I hope that they are not going to divorce.* Florette has been relating similar incidents concerning her parents' arguments. *Is it the same?* Tata Fanny and Tonton Georges are constantly threatening to divorce. Tonton Georges is physically abusing and terrorizing Tata Fanny, as well as Florette, who pleads with her father, literally on her knees, to stop this behavior. It is reassuring that this is not my experience. Interestingly, Georges does not strike Marc (his son).

*As if this situation is not bad enough! Now, there is someone else at home, to share Papa's attention*: Mania, Maman's unmarried cousin from Lithuania. Mania managed to escape with the problems in Kedaniai having worsened. Maman cannot refuse to accept her. They grew up together. *But I really don't need her to be here with us, not when Papa and Maman are at each other's throat.* Two women in the same kitchen cause friction.

Arguments are frequent. Mania worships Papa. I sense it, and I hate her. Physically not very attractive, she has a big nose and a wide mouth with a prominent gold tooth in front and is vulgar and forever plucking her eyebrows, to complete the ensemble. Some stylish clothing including a beaded flapper dress and evening bag (which I secretly admire) are brought from the *shtetl. Believe it or not.* I want to borrow them to play dress up but am refused. This is another reason to hate her.

"Maman, quand est-ce qu'elle part?" (Mom, when is she leaving?) *"Mania bleibt mit uns* (Mania stays), she has nowhere else to go," explains Maman. "Papa has work for her at the factory." *Good. I won't see her during the day. But she'll be with Papa.* As this is written, so many years later, the intense resentment disrupting my family's privacy remains strong. This animosity, already felt in childhood, only festered as time went on.

The air raids continue. Father is getting edgy despite an outward cavalier attitude. The news is not encouraging. Hitler invades Denmark and Norway in April 1940, followed by Belgium and Luxemburg. In early May, Papa decides to send us to Cap-Breton, a small town near Biarritz, near the Spanish border. He remains in Paris with Mania, hoping the French Army will halt the German advance at the Maginot Line, as occurred at the river Marne in World War I. At that time Parisian taxis, filled with men of all ages, were sent to the front, to help stop the Germans, which succeeded. Not now. Maman and I leave by train before German bombs destroy the railway system.

Nowadays, the word *exode* in French refers to the summer departure of Parisians on vacation. Then, it probably derives from the national "Exodus" which starts on June 6, 1940, from

Paris, and becomes even more massive when Paris is declared an "Open City" (one not to be bombed) on June 11. People are unable to use railways, which have been damaged by the bombardments. The populace leaves by car, bike, and on foot, depending on their financial means, taking with them as many possessions as possible. The wealthy exit first. Tonton Georges, Papa, Mania, and Max finally abandon Paris in a car belonging to Claude Magnin, Max's son-in-law, who also departs. Maman, Anale, Max's wife, their daughter Jeanine, and I are already settled in Cap-Breton, a charming little town on the southwest coast of the Atlantic, to be soon joined by Florette, Marc, and Tata Fanny, as well as her sisters and their brood. It feels like a vacation, living together in the same house. Anale inhabits another with her daughter. Tata Régine and her family have remained in Paris because they cannot afford the trip. Every day is spent at the beach; a repetition of the vacation in Sables d'Olonne. Florette and I play, unaware of the grave situation, and take gymnastic lessons. Goat cheese with bread is discovered for breakfast.

Papa is sorely missed and repeatedly inquired about. This seems to trigger Maman's sobbing. Tata Fanny tries to console and reassure her, in vain.

One afternoon, Mania, who became separated from him and the others on the way, arrives first. She has lost much weight, and her clothes hang loosely from her thin body. Ravenously hungry, she eats as if there were no tomorrow, interrupted only for a sip of *tchai* or to talk of recent events. *Paris, Ville Ouverte* (the Open City), meant that the Germans were closing in. Claude's car ran out of gasoline in Orléans, and there was none available to purchase. The city was bombed by the Germans. Masses of people were on the bridges and roads. Farmers, with their belongings loaded on horse-driven carts, were followed by their farm animals. Mania became separated, walking southwest alone, until soldiers provided her a lift to Cap-Breton. (19)

There is no news from Papa, Tonton Georges, Max, and Claude.

In July, two months after our arrival in Cap-Breton, our fathers are leaning out the window, smiling and waving as we return from the beach. I run to the house, screaming for joy, "Papa, Papa!" and leap in his arms, at the door. It feels so good as he holds me tightly. I feel safe again, reassured by the familiar scent of his *Gitane* cigarettes. *Papa looks tired and has also lost weight.*

Suddenly there is a cry in the hallway. Florette stands near her father, blushing. Tears are running down her cheeks.

"What's the matter?" asks Papa with a frown.

Tonton Georges, impassive, declares that all is well, but I am suspicious because of past events. Florette tells me later that still fearful, felt paralyzed on seeing her father once again, she did not greet him with enthusiasm and was struck in the face. Tata Fanny stands there tearfully, incapable of action. Appalled, we ignore this frightening and repulsive man. Everyone is tense and embarrassed, but Papa does not intervene, believing, as related much later, that it was a family matter and not his concern. At the time, I looked at him, imploringly: *"Do something, Papa!"* His silence disappointed me.

Papa recounts his adventures at dinner. After Mania was lost in the confusion of the Orléans bombardment, it has taken a month to travel from Paris to Cap-Breton. They walked or hitchhiked with retreating army convoys on the remaining distance south, finding shelter where able, sometimes under heavy German bombardment of the countryside. The resulting sights were horrible: dead bodies or parts thereof lay strewn on the roadway. Rumors ran amok in the cafés en route. Spies were everywhere. No one could be trusted. A story was told of a Wehrmacht officer disguised as a nun. People were in flight, pillaging along the way. Liberated criminals, the insane, lost cats, dogs, and cows wandered about, homeless and hungry. This was the image of France during the summer exodus of 1940. (19)

Max and Claude rejoined their wives in another house in Cap-Breton. The "vacation" for me happily continued, content being with parents and close relatives. Fanny was self-educated, read extensively, and shared similar tastes with Papa, which made her special. She would sing, read stories, and play with us. Florette envied the affection then bestowed on me by Papa but, nevertheless, shared the comfort of his lap while listening to the marvelous stories of la Comtesse de Ségur. Years later, Florette confided the belief that Papa had been in love with her mother, which did not surprise me. There was a great affinity between them.

The children were unaware that at the end of June 1940 the armistice was already signed. Two areas were delineated in France: the Occupied (Northern) Zone including Paris and directly under control by the Nazis, and the Unoccupied (Southern) Zone or Free France with Vichy as its administrative center, directed by the collaborationist government of Maréchal Pétain and Pierre Laval. The Vichy government consisted of individuals seeking revenge. Catholics who remembered the Dreyfus Affair, right-wingers fearful of communism, patriots frustrated by the lies of incompetent politicians, and middle-class bourgeois impoverished by international monetary disasters. Opportunists replaced the politicians at that time. Parliamentary democracy was set aside; totalitarianism was the rule of law. It was generally believed that Maréchal Philippe Pétain, the hero of Verdun during World War I, would again be France's savior and replace chaos with order.

The masses who had not met him personally were impressed by the Maréchal, but the politicians, at first abashed and curious, were soon disappointed by his reserve. He was eighty-four years old but still believed together with the old French guard of 1917, in the merit of age, and God's intervention on behalf of France. (20)

Petain's henchman, Pierre Laval, was in fact the deus ex machina of the fall of the Third Republic and the change in the French regime. Son of a simple butcher and café owner, despite humble origins, he rose in the ranks to become the actual head of the Vichy government from 1942 to 1944. (21)

As Hitler visited Paris, Jews in Biarritz and other neighboring cities were attempting to obtain visas for Spain and Portugal. Our little group discussed what to do next in the warm evenings on the terrace. We considered trying to escape like the others or return to Paris. Why not leave France at that time when it was still possible? This was a query I wish could be posed to Father. Retrospectively, I believe he wanted to return to the shoe factory in Paris, rationalizing, reconciling, and in fact regrettably ignoring, along with many others, the reality of events. Was it apathy or fear? I think it was the latter. Where would we have gone? There were no relatives in the United States, except the Hertsteins, who faced similar problems. The comparatively primitive life in Palestine, as it was then called, before it became Israel, was not attractive. Attachment to France, and perennial optimism, made Father impervious to the very serious situation.

German soldiers who came to Biarritz and Cap-Breton with their cameras and smiles were very "correct," polite, and paid for everything. Yet, they were referred to with despise as *Les Boches* or *Krauts*.

One day, playing on the sand at the beach with Florette and Maman nearby, I was approached by a German soldier, smiling, candy in hand. Having frequently heard this disparaging insult, to Maman's horror, I blurt out, "Je n' prends rien d'un sale Boche" (I take nothing from a dirty Kraut). Florette throws back her head and bursts out laughing, and Maman, unsmiling and trembling, drags us hurriedly back to the house.

This is also the day when the entire family decides to go back to Paris. If the Germans are here in Cap-Breton, near Spain . . . *et bien!* There is no point in remaining.

The extended vacation was finished.

# CHAPTER VII

## MARECHAL PETAIN, SAVIOR OF FRANCE

The signing of the armistice was very painful for many Frenchmen. They were demoralized by the *Blitzkrieg*, the swift, overpowering German offensive. Some committed suicide rather than face the shame of surrender. Others left for North Africa to continue the struggle, or like Général de Gaulle, for Great Britain to establish the Government of Free France. Soldiers deserted or assassinated those officers who wanted to continue the fight, preferring to be captured. Some officers abandoned their men. It was the total collapse of the army, the population, and the government. Only a few stray airmen, sailors, and foot-soldiers answered the call of de Gaulle in England. (22)

Two million Frenchmen were prisoners when the armistice was signed. Demobilized, Uncle Jean returned, but Uncle Emile did not. Peace, on German terms, soon followed, and at what price! Nazi power was felt throughout France in varying degree, and especially in Paris. Curfew extended from 11:00 PM to 7:00 AM. Bread, sugar, and noodles were rationed. The Germans requisitioned food for their troops. The price of fruit and vegetables markedly increased and were obtained either with ration cards or on the black market. Chocolate was nonexistent (a Hershey bar given to me by an American soldier was my first taste of chocolate at age seventeen in 1949). Rutabagas (turnips) and *topinambours* (Jerusalem Artichokes) replaced potatoes. (23) Maman tried in vain to make me eat them; their names just turned me off, reminding me of threatening plants grown in fantasy gardens. The German word *Ersatz* (substitution) was used jokingly to describe almost everything on the market including cookies (which tasted horrible) distributed in school. Maman, as with other women, colored her legs with tan dye to simulate silk stockings, which were not available. Shoes had wooden soles since leather was in short supply.

Night life had resumed, mostly for the German occupants, and their collaborationists. The Folies-Bergère, the Opéra, and the Opéra-Comique offered their spectacles to some Parisians while others silently lined up for bread, at bakeries. Gasoline was reserved primarily for the occupying forces and the wealthy who could afford black market prices. Many Parisians used the metro and bicycles. It was not safe to talk to strangers or even acquaintances. Informers were everywhere.

Although many projects were required to rebuild the country, unemployment was extensive. Women were among the first victims, having to accept menial jobs in order to survive. Jobless Frenchmen were offered work in Germany. There was censorship of newspapers and the mail. Banks were taken over by the enemy. Alsace-Lorraine was annexed by Germany and inhabitants of French origin, expelled. Trade unions were dissolved and universities closed. The Germans ordered a census of Jews in the Occupied Zone. They were forbidden from the medical, legal, and teaching professions. Racist insults were legal. (23) The collaborationist government was centered in Vichy, a health resort known for its mineral water and its therapeutic procedures. As mentioned before, the French believed (some still do) that drinking Vichy water was valuable in treating liver diseases. French and foreign bourgeoisie had visited this resort which is situated in central France in the new Free Zone. Bordeaux had been the first choice as capital, but Maréchal Pétain and the government opted for Vichy because its spacious hotels were able to house many administrative departments. The defeat of 1940 also resulted in the destruction of democratic institutions of the Third Republic. Cause for the disaster had to be found. The Popular Front with its socialistic programs, and its Jewish leader, Léon Blum, became scapegoats. Blum was tried, initially imprisoned in France, and subsequently sent to a concentration camp. "Loose" behavior including alcohol, night life, and short skirts were also blamed for the debacle. General decadence had weakened the French people (it was said). (23)

However, the *Juifs* (Jews) were considered the primary cause of the defeat of France. My first experience with anti-Semitism occurred one day when Mania tearfully rushed into the apartment, short of breath. Someone in the grocery store had shouted to her, "Rentre chez toi, Abraham" (Go home, Abraham). We also feared the *concierge* of our apartment who was identified as a *yente* by my mother and a *pipelette* by my father, pejorative epithets referring to "a gossip." Madame Tardu, on hearing us approach, would wait at the door of her *loge* (apartment) for *une petite conversation*, usually wearing a dirty old dark housedress hidden by a soiled, torn apron; large feet encased in rolled socks and grimy slippers. With smiling lips but cold dark eyes, she would tenderly caress the huge gray cat which hissed as we passed by. Maman never failed to stop and chat, saying, "Bonjour Madame Tardu, ça va?" (Good day, Madame Tardu, how are you doing?)

"Eh! Que voulez-vous, Madame Henri, on se défend! Avec tout c'qui s'passe maint'nant" (Eh! Madame Henri, we manage! With what's going on now!), she said with a Gallic shrug, unsuccessfully attempting to prod Maman into conversation about the political situation. My mother did not trust her. Afterwards, Maman would admonish me to ignore, "Asa Antisemitke! Asa paskudniak! A chalerie soll ihr nemmen!" (Such an anti-Semite! Such a bitch! She should get cholera!).

The optician chain *Lissac* had as its motto: "Lissac n'est pas Isaac" (Lissac is not Isaac). In the subway, a poster presented a hideous face with hooked nose and chin, the caption reading: "Le Juif Süss." It was an advertisement for a vicious propaganda film produced by Goebbels (Hitler's propaganda minister) and very distressing. When returning home, my father was asked for an explanation. "Some people don't like Jews," said Papa, "and they'll do anything to show us in a bad light." In *Le Juif Süss*, history was sorely misrepresented by the Nazis, who portrayed the main character, Oppenheimer, as a rich and greedy man who overthrew the government, drove a young girl to suicide, provoked a popular uprising, and was finally tried and hung. The populace cheered. After the war, a more accurate account was found. In Würtenberg in 1730, Süss Oppenheimer, who considered (himself) Jewish, was counselor to the duke . . . and then later discovered that he was actually Gentile.

Maréchal Pétain was regarded as the savior who would reestablish discipline and transform the institutions of the Third Republic. *Travail, Famille, Patrie* (Work, Family, Fatherland) was the motto, and the Frankish Axe, at one time, the weapon of Clovis (the first French king), the logo. New moral values were developed to encourage the ideals of work, family, and above all, patriotism. Teachers were required to recite an oath to the Maréchal. At school, we sang:

> "Maréchal, nous voilà (Marechal, here we are),
> "Devant toi (Before you),
> "Le Sauveur de la France (The Savior of France) . . ."

*The Marseillaise* was also sung frequently and with fervor in school. On graduating from the *Ecole Maternelle* to the *Ecole Elémentaire*, my only friends were cousins Florette and François. Shy and withdrawn, there was nevertheless a young friend in school, Fernande Terron, perhaps because we shared common first names, interests, and were of similar size. Maman placed a wide ribbon in her hair. Although we played at each other's home, our mothers did not socialize. Fernande was Catholic, which did not matter in the relationship. When the time arrived to leave Paris, sadly we promised to write and see one another after the war. An old photograph is the only remaining memory of Fernande Terron. The photographer had placed us in the same pensive position, sitting at a table, book in one hand, head leaning on a forearm, unsmiling, as if realizing that the separation was forever. Both being good students, we sometimes studied together. However, certain questions puzzled me, which were not shared with her, especially in history. This was a favorite subject. I memorized all the important dates, even those which did not interest me. Who cared about the fall of the Holy Roman Empire? However, King Louis IX's canonization was disturbing. What made him Saint Louis? It was well known that he loved his mother Blanche de Castille, performed many good works, and washed people's feet to prove his humility. So what? I loved my mother too, did not wash anyone's feet, but did not hate Christians. St. Louis hated the Jews. What about the other saints? Saint Geneviève, who protected Paris from the Huns, Saint Jeanne d'Arc, who saved France from the English. Did they like us? Stories of the Crusades and the Inquisition were frightening. Had Henri IV given religious freedom to the Jews as well as the Protestants with the Edit de Nantes? (As I later learned, he did not.) I did not dare ask; the teacher might become angry and put a dunce hat on my head. It seemed all so strange. Although these questions kept my mind in turmoil, they were not verbally expressed. Papa's answers were not satisfying. According to him, the French were infallible; France was the land of milk and honey and the country of freedom, despite all the hardships it placed upon the Jews. This feeling of being an outsider was enhanced by the history books which described the Gauls as our "forefathers." Somehow, my peaceful, loving father could not be readily related to these powerful Celtic warlords. Assimilation to Papa also included acceptance of the status quo with historical French anti-Semitism notwithstanding.

Papa especially liked the cinema. Saturday night was "movie night." French films reflected the populist mood of the nation. He truly appreciated the nuances of French culture interpreted in these films by actors such as Jean Gabin, so attractive in his portrayal of the working-class *mauvais garçon* (bad boy), Arletty, Maurice Chevalier, and Mistinguett, and their *accent faubourien*

(Parisian street accent). Father could repeat the dialogue of Raimu and Fernandel from a film of Marcel Pagnol almost verbatim, chuckling all the while, particularly, the belote card-game scene from *César*, one of Pagnol's trilogy. The inimitable throaty retort of Arletty to Louis Jouvet, "Atmosphère! . . ." (in *Hôtel du Nord*) is unforgettable. I accompanied my parents to most films, even double features including American movies, although dubbed in French. There was *Zorro*, who returned regularly in exciting adventures. *Frankenstein* was so horrifying that I crawled under the seat to escape the monster who, fortunately, appeared to die by incineration or in a bath of sulfuric acid . . . only to be revived again for the next production! Although these films resulted in nightmares, my parents, surprisingly, ignored them and took me anyway. The dos and don'ts of child psychology were not yet in vogue.

During the Occupation, German films (including *Le Juif Süss*) also appeared in France; Musicals with Zarah Leander and Marika Rokk were among the favorites, especially the film on the life of Tchaikovsky entitled *Es war eine rauschende Ballnacht* or *Pages Immortelles* (French title), by the German director Carl Froehlich, which introduced me to this composer's music. Tchaikovsky might perhaps have been amused (or annoyed) at this interpretation, since the film implies a liaison with a dancer, despite his alleged homosexuality.

Dancing became important in my life after viewing Marika Rokk performing Tchaikovsky's brilliant waltz. At Nadine's wedding in 1939, the fashionable dances of the time such as "la Kukaratcha" or "The Lambeth Walk" were thrilling, though I was only seven. Music seemed to flow through my limbs which would move and whirl in harmony. Feeling dizzy but joyful, I could not sit still. The guests thought I looked "so cute" in my ball gown.

Though struggling with Burgmuller and other beginners' piano exercises, Madame Tryvous appreciated my talent for music and encouraged Maman to introduce me to Madame Preobrajenskaia, former prima ballerina to the Czar, now ballet teacher par excellence, who had escaped the Bolshevik Revolution. Madame was now instructing *Les Petits Rats* (little rats or young ballet students) of the Paris Opera and coaching its prima ballerinas. One afternoon, Maman, Madame Tryvous, and *petite* me, arrived at the Place Clichy, Studio Wacker. The studio no longer exists. At the time, it was situated above a Playel Piano Store. I imagined acquiring the baby grand piano in the window (which did not happen). Many famous artists studied ballet with Madame Preobrajenskaia. Michèle Morgan, the actress, took classes with her to prepare for a film, as did Tony Lander of the Netherlands Ballet with whom I reminisced many years later in Salt Lake City (where my daughter danced with Ballet West). The tortuous stairway and rhythmic piano music led us to the dim dressing rooms. Young girls were transforming themselves, like chrysalides, shedding their street clothes for black leotards, white socks, and black slippers. Hair arranged in a chignon and voilà! They looked different, graceful, and elegant. Observing them with curiosity and envy, I fell in love with ballet at that moment, in spite of the dinginess of the room and the odor of sweat and unwashed bodies. Crossing the dressing room toward the sound of music, Madame Tryvous, smiling, opened the door to the magic kingdom, a large hall with mirrors on one wall, and a pianist and chairs near another. It was the end of a class, and Madame Preobrajenskaia approached. A tiny woman with a wrinkled face and a smile that hid her decayed teeth (*poor oral hygiene and nutrition seemed to have ruined many European teeth*), Madame was wearing a long brown jumper and tights with a white shirt. Brown ballet slippers completed the outfit. My senses were acutely moved by the sights and sounds; butterflies seemed to flitter in my stomach.

Madame's welcome was most generous and warm, kissing me on both cheeks, as she then proceeded to do the same to Madame Tryvous and to Maman, while gesticulating and exclaiming shrilly in Russian. It was all so bewildering and fascinating, particularly the young women and girls warming up at the barre and dancing on the center of the floor. After this visit, Maman bought a complete outfit for me. The big ribbon remained in place for ballet class. Soon, I was pirouetting with the rest of them, determined to become the next Anna Pavlova. *Rrras, dwah, trrree, tcheteerreh* (one, two, three, four) would roll from Madame's thin lips. The truly versatile pianist could play any musical piece and simultaneously follow Madame's instructions.

Madame Preobrajenskaia, although advanced in age, was still able to demonstrate the steps. I became her favorite student and, as such, would be placed in the first row. Soon, at the age of eight, permission was granted to wear pointe shoes, another honor. These shoes were cherished during the entire war and worn sometimes, just to recall these treasured balletic moments.

It was exhilarating to piqué, turn, from one corner of the room to the other, exalted by the music and the exercises, during Madame's class. When the music started, gravity seemed to disappear. I felt like a bird in flight. It is interesting to note in this regard that some classical ballets use birds as central subjects. I dreamed of dancing in Tchaikovsky's *Swan Lake*, or Stravinsky's *Firebird*, but most of all, Saint-Saens' *Death of the Swan*. Pavlova's, and much later Makarova's graceful arms, resembled the broken wings of the dying swan. In the last bars of the variation, as the ballerina slowly sinks to the floor, one leg bent beneath, head pitifully nestled within her arms, beautiful hands crossed over the other outstretched leg, pointed slipper in exact alignment. These images are sketched indelibly in memory.

The prima ballerina of the time, la Toumanova, occasionally joined us. Admiringly, I danced proudly nearby, swearing one day to follow in her footsteps Maman would observe the class quietly in a corner, smiling and *kvelling* (swelling) with pride, particularly proud when Madame approached to compliment my progress. In an adjacent hall, dancers were rehearsing a Liszt rhapsody, wearing red boots and Gypsy peasant costumes. One day, fascinated, after observing the rehearsal for a while, I memorized the dance and performed it at home for my parents, while humming the music.

"Oh, Maman, promise me a Gypsy outfit! Please! You didn't make me a Sablaise outfit, remember?"

"Oy, Fernandele, vos villst du fun mir? Bon! Bon! Soll sine azey. Du vest hobben azey a costum" (Oh! Little Fernande, what do you want from me? OK! OK! You'll have such a costume).

I implored Papa to make red boots. The Gypsy costume never materialized, nor did the boots.

Uncle Isaac's unexpected visit in the middle of the night, accompanied by the two French policemen, previously described, interrupted "my budding dance career." Madame Preobrajenskaia was preparing me for entrance to the Opera Ballet Company as *un petit rat*. I recall passing the opera with Maman, hoping that one day the dream would come true, imagining the audience applauding the great ballerina dancing Tchaikovsky's waltz. My chosen stage name was to be Natasha Alexandrovna. (Natasha was one of Maman's Lithuanian nieces, and Alexandrovna, her Russian maiden name.) The last ballet class occurred the day prior to departure for the Demarcation Line. Madame, recognizing my talent, sorrowfully said goodbye and embraced me, which never was forgotten. These memories sustained me during four long years of occupation.

After the war, returning to Studios Wacker at age fourteen, the basic steps were remembered. However, dancing nearby were graceful little girls with a hundred-eighty-degree turnout. The reflection in the mirror revealed a plump, clumsy, and angry teenager. Feeling very self-conscious, I was unable to perform, my turnout nonexistent. Worst of all, Madame approached the barre to correct my position. Looking intensely at one another, I then realized that she did not recognize me (*moi, son étudiante favorite*). The past was gone and beyond redemption. My throat constricted, and I fought back the tears. Still wearing the same jumper, shirt, and slippers, Madame appeared no older, except for a few more facial lines, her brown hair streaked with gray. A dance career was never encouraged by my father and seemed too difficult in any case. School lasted until 5:00 PM, to be followed by a rush to ballet class, and then completion of the day's homework. I attended a few classes. The shock and disappointment were such, when not recognized by Madame, that the old pointe shoes were discarded, and I never returned to Studios Wacker. However, the love of ballet still remains although I never saw a performance before the war. Subsequently, viewing the talents of Maria and Rosella Hightower of the *Ballets du Marquis de Cuevas*, Zizi Jeanmaire of the *Ballets Roland Petit* in the 1950s, and the incomparable Natalia Makarova of the *American Ballet Theatre*, later in the 1970s, among many others, was simultaneously exhilarating and emotionally painful.

*Mamale*, I think you would be most happy to know that much later, this affection for ballet was passed on to your granddaughters. Deborah became a classical ballerina with a national ballet company for several years; Vera, a modern dancer, choreographer, and cinematographer. Emulating you, I "encouraged" the children to learn a musical instrument. It was an unsuccessful project with Deborah. Vera played the harp and Marc the trumpet . . . for a while, anyway. It was not my intent to press the issue. However, retrospectively, I am grateful that you did "force" me to continue piano lessons. Now, I play for pleasure and relaxation.

Madame Preobrajenskaia lived a long time. I saw her one evening at the opera, applauding Yvette Chauviré in *Le Cygne Noir* Variation. I thought, *It could have been me.* Whenever viewing ballet, my chest tightens with regret.

Yvette Chauviré was beautiful.

Sadly, I never saw Madame Tryvous again; she died in Auschwitz.

# CHAPTER VIII

## SWASTIKA AND AXE OF VICHY

The first roundup of foreign Jews began in Paris in May 1941, in the *XIe Arrondissement* (Eleventh district) near Avenue Parmentier, close to our apartment, which included Uncle Isaac's arrest. This nocturnal visit by the two French policemen galvanized Father to send us away. Max Ochsman's son-in-law, Claude Magnin, was to be the interim factory's manager. Claude's wife remained with him in Paris and escaped deportation because she was married to a Christian. Claude promised Papa to take proper care of the factory and to send money, every month. As my mother would say, "A nechtige toog!" (a dark day). Funds were never sent. Papa wrote to him several times during the war without result, finally sending him a sarcastic note: "Dîtes-moi merde, mais dîtes-moi quelque chose!" (Say shit, but say something). This missive was also ignored.

After the "misadventure" of the Demarcation Line, my companions and I arrived safely in Aix-les-Bains in the summer of 1941. Papa had heard that Aix-les-Bains was a lovely town under the relatively benign Italian occupation and influence.

Aix-Les-Bains is situated in the Alps, in the *Département* of the Savoie. It is a pretty city on the shore of the Lac du Bourget. The nineteenth-century poet Lamartine, whose lover was forever lost there, immortalized the "Lake" with a poem: *Le Lac*. "O Temps! Suspends ton vol!" (O Time! Stop your flight!) is a famous line;

time passes but nature remains the same, implacable. The Alps border the lake, and in the distance, one can see *La Dent du Chat* (the Cat's tooth), a high peak, separating Aix from Yenne, our future residence. The *Mont Revard* (altitude: 1,500 meters), another mountain, dominates the landscape on the opposite side of the lake. Returning to Aix-Les-Bains after the war, I noticed that little appeared to have changed except the casino, a man-made, indoor playground for the rich, which now looked decrepit, and in need of restoration. The odor of sulfur from the natural springs still permeated the air.

This spa attracted the wealthy and royalty from the turn of the century until the war. It was an elegant crowd, many British, who inhabited pretty villas on the hills, and religiously followed their doctor's directives for hot sulfur baths and water cures. In the evenings, they visited the casino, to gamble, dance, or listen to famous entertainers such as Mistinguett, the most popular female French vocalist of the time (prior to Edith Piaf). The favorite tune, "Paris, c'est une blonde," was interpreted in her inimitable smoky and raspy voice which was greeted with wild, sustained applause. My parents took me to hear her sing after the war, at the same casino where I drank my first glass of champagne. Nowadays, the casino is a poor replica of the gambling hotels in Las Vegas. The spa stills functions but is no longer exclusive.

On June 10, 1940, the Savoyards believe that they have been "stabbed in the back" when war is declared by Mussolini. The French Général Cartier and the Alps Army make a stand, but the Rhône bridges are blown up and Lyon is declared an Open City. The Germans, in order to support their ally, send two units of troops to Chambéry and Grenoble. Two of the Rhône bridges escape destruction, and the Germans are able to enter Chambéry, the *Département*'s capital. Aix-les-Bains, approximately twenty-five kilometers (fifteen miles) distant, is also declared an Open City. The Germans pass through and are welcomed by the mayor, Monsieur Dussuel, and his adjunct, Monsieur Chevalier, with open arms. The Aixois observe them march by. The shelling of the neighboring village of Grésine is within earshot. The German soldiers fill the stores and at the *Redoute*, a famous restaurant, 450 pastries are requisitioned. They have not tasted chocolate or cakes for the past three years. Their army is motorized. No soldier walks. A French locksmith, Monsieur Magnin, observes: "These people have ten years experience on us, with their efficient brakes and odorless gasoline; while among our troops, cannons are pulled by mules or horses, the (mobile military) kitchens are unstable, our men walk for kilometers carrying more than thirty kilograms of military junk or drive in commercial cars with loud and colorful logos." (24)

The Germans occupied Aix-les-Bains for twelve days, leaving on July 5, 1940. On November 11, 1942, the Italians returned once again and occupied the Savoie and the Côte d'Azur. They protected the Jews and avoided arresting the *Maquis* (French Résistance).Unfortunately, in March 1943, the Demarcation Line ceased to exist, and the Germans reoccupied the territory in September 1943.

Upon our arrival in Aix from Vierzon, it was quiet. There were no Germans. We rented a room in a hotel and spent the first days becoming familiarized with the surroundings. The hotel faced a beautiful, tree-lined park, elegantly arranged with brilliant flower beds. Maman and I would deeply inhale the scent of the flowers and freshly cut grass, which sometimes wafted through the open windows of our room. Afternoons were spent in taking photographs while strolling in the park. *La Rotonde* restaurant was around the corner of our hotel, and occasionally, we had tea on the terrace. Papa and Max joined us several weeks later. Although inhabiting the same hotel, there was no social contact with Anale and her husband because of Maman's discontent and distrust of their son-in-law, who was now in charge of the factory.

My parents leased a modest house on the hill near the beautiful villas which we so admired when descending to the town. In the opposite direction, the roadway led to the summit of Mont Revard, which had downhill skiing and was very popular with the Aixois. When winter came, Papa and Maman could not resist my pleas, and on a sunny day we took the *téléphérique* to the top. There, a beautiful panoramic view of the region awaited. In the distance, the snow-covered, steep slopes of Mont Blanc rose majestically. The family had never skied before; nevertheless, Father happily rented the equipment. Unfortunately, the skis could not be properly attached to the boots, and instead of skiing, we simply posed and fell down anyway, the memory of which is captured on cherished photographs which still bring a smile.

Papa bought me a tricycle, soon to be replaced by a two-wheeled bike. It felt safe with him holding on to the seat which one afternoon was suddenly released. It was liberating, coasting down the hill against the wind, without falling. Of course, pushing the bike uphill was an ordeal. It gave me pause to observe the Hotel Albion more carefully, an elegant cream-colored structure which had been a prewar favorite haunt of the British bourgeoisie. In 1978, my husband, children and I spent the day at the Albion, had a gourmet lunch, and swam in the pool. When we returned in 2000, the hotel had been replaced by an apartment house.

The summer of 1940 was pleasant, bathing and lounging in the sun, on the pure white sand of the Lac du Bourget's man-made beach. The most traumatic experience then was learning to swim. The instructor threw me in the lake, tethered to a long leash. I plummeted into the cold water, the cord around my waist pulled me up, gasping, teeth noisily clacking. I learned quickly. There was no choice. Sink or swim.

This complacent lifestyle was clearly not warranted, given the events that shortly unfolded. Many years later, while relating these events to my students, the following obvious question was raised: "How could you live like that, while all this went on around you?" Nowadays, journalists "embedded" with our troops in Iraq provided a detailed account of events as they happened in real time, as we participated, sitting glued to the TV set. Then, my parents were apparently unaware or did not fully comprehend the truly dangerous circumstances, in part because of censorship of the newspapers and radio programming, and quite probably, due to a conscious desire to block out such troubling thoughts. In any case, Jews were not permitted to own a radio. Father, the eternal optimist, was certain that this situation would be short lived. Savings were spent primarily for rent and food. Papa had to exchange gold Louis for French money. We lived frugally but were never hungry. I don't recall purchasing clothing during the war. Maman continued to sew mine manually. My parents' clothes were worn till threadbare. However, shoes, which were brought along from the factory, were plentiful. Sturdier, warmer footwear, with soles made of wood and cork needed for the cold mountain winters, were purchased locally.

Nevertheless, the Nazis and the Vichy Government were not satisfied since tight control of southern France was lacking. It was known that the Jews were fleeing Paris to escape the raids. France is administratively divided in *Départements*, and these subdivided in *Préfectures*. The seat of our Préfecture was in Chambéry. By order of Vichy, the Préfectures declared that all Jews had to choose a registered domicile. They called it *Résidance Forcée*, or Forced Residence. Consider a released prisoner having to report to a parole officer. This was simply an administrative tool to determine the whereabouts of the Jews at all times. Hollerith, an IBM subsidiary, had collaborated with the Nazis and the Vichy Government to provide a punch-card system to carry out Jewish registration and census, which greatly facilitated their deportation to concentration camps. (25) The Jews could not remain in Aix because Chambéry's Préfecture had assigned specific villages for this forced residence. Although it is surprising that such privilege was permitted, our choices included Moutiers, Belley, and Yenne.

Papa first made some inquiries. One of his former wholesale clients, a Monsieur Blanchin, had a retail shoe store in Yenne and informed the manager, Monsieur Chagnon. Papa met the Chagnons, immediately developed a rapport with the family, and was struck by their honesty, decency, and common sense. Father decided to rent a house in Yenne. Leaving Aix-les-Bains immediately, we arrived in Yenne at the end of 1941 and remained there for four years. Fortunately, Father made the right decision because when the Germans returned in 1943, Moutiers and

Bellay were occupied. Arrests were made of Jews and maquisards. Yenne was never occupied, although periodically raided.

At the end of the summer of 1942, when the Nazi train transports from Drancy to Auschwitz began to increase, aunts Fanny and Suzanne decided to come to Yenne. I was delighted. Florette would be here, in six weeks. My impatience annoyed Papa and Maman. This short period seemed like six years, since I had no friends in school. Their arrival in Yenne remains one of the happiest days of my life. When they had settled in the house my father had found for them, we dined together. Tata Fanny informed us of the Allied bombardments in Le Havre and Rouen, which she had learned from Catholic friends and the demoralizing newsreel propaganda. The German soldiers were depicted as great heroes and the Allies as cruel monsters. Jews were shown as filthy, rapidly multiplying vermin, destined to destroy the well-meaning Aryan, Christian populations of France and Germany. To our horror, we learned that during the Gestapo raids or *rafles,* the Jews were cruelly torn from their homes, with few personal belongings. Apartments were looted, smashed and then, officially sealed.

Their experience at the Demarcation Line was equally as frightening as it had been for us. Traveling by train in one compartment sat Fanny and her mother-in-law, who spoke only Yiddish, and in another were Suzanne, baby Michel, Florette, and little Marc, who was only three. There was only one *passeur* for the entire group, a Gentile woman, Max's mistress, who had false papers and was supposedly Florette and Marc's mother. Fanny moved back and forth between the two compartments, reminding Grandma not to utter a word. Marc was taught to address his mother as "Madame" and Max's mistress as "Maman." He otherwise kept quiet. The grandmother was not required to speak at all. As youngsters, it was inherently understood that silence meant "survival." Fortuitously, the group had no problem at the checkpoint.

News of the remaining family was painfully divulged. Aunt Suzanne burst into tears; her husband had been deported. Fanny's youngest sister Jeannette and her husband had departed for Pau (in central France) with their children.

"Do you have any news from the Blumenthals and the Spitzers?" asked Maman.

"Eveline and Isidore Spitzer were deported. The Blumenthals, as well as Nadine, Marthe, and Vladek, went to Cannes," Fanny grimly answered.

Aunt Régine, her husband Max, and François were arrested in the Vel d'Hiv raid and deported, while Thérèse, so disliked by her stepmother, had been sent to summer camp, thus escaping deportation. Thérèse remained with Tata Fanny for a short period of time, then left for Belgium to join her father's relatives.

"Elle se rongeait les ongles et pleurait durant la nuit" (She bit her nails and cried at night), remembered Florette.

"She was scared," added Fanny, sighing. "Everyone was scared. During the day, it was mandatory to wear the yellow Star of David on outer clothing. I didn't want to leave the apartment, but food had to be obtained." Even that was restricted to certain hours, between 3:00 and 4:00 PM. At night, in hiding, they slept in a small room on the fifth floor, ordinarily used by house servants. Noise of any kind was minimized since the fourth-floor neighbor was an informer who already had denounced other people.

The situation had become untenable for everyone, but especially for Jews. An ordinance forbade them from participating in any profession, cultural or sport activity, or from owning a radio or a telephone . . . everything that enriches life! Food was scarce, even with ration coupons. Whatever was available, albeit in the countryside, was sent to Germany, while many people in France were starving.

The situation significantly worsened in July, with the Vel d'Hiv raid.

Eichmann had arrived in Paris to organize the deportation of Jews.

The Vélodrome d'Hiver, or Vel d'Hiv in abbreviation, was an indoor bicycle arena. Seven thousand Jews, including four thousand children, were incarcerated there for a week in the scorching July heat. Simultaneously, an additional six thousand other Jews were detained in Drancy. A mother who had already escaped the Polish pogroms threw herself out the window with her child rather than be taken. The latrines were insufficient; human waste flowed from the stepped rows of the stadium. People stumbled in the filth-ridden mud while others were overcome by the heat, illness, and lack of water. Only two physicians and a few Red Cross nurses were available for the sick. (26) Friends warned Fanny to leave Paris.

She did.

"C'est incroyable" (It's unbelievable), said Papa. "We are totally unaware of these terrible events since they were not published in the local newspapers, *Le Petit Dauphinois* and the *Allobroges*, a communist paper. These are dangerous times, and the family feels more secure together."

Maman grabbed Fanny's hand, squeezed it warmly, and said, "What's happening to Georges, your husband?"

"Il fricote probablement avec les Boches" (He probably messes around with the Krauts). "We neither saw or spoke with him before our departure and hope never to have any contact again."

"Soll er gehn in Drerd," summed up Maman.

Georges' mother, a *verbissene* (embittered) old woman showing early signs of senility, grimaced as the story unfolded. Despite her unpleasant personality, she was treated with kindness and respect by Tata Fanny. My most vivid recollections of this person were her clacking teeth (couldn't stand the noise) and physical abuse of Florette's black-and-white kitten, *Moustique* (Mosquito).

Sitting near the old woman, Aunt Suzanne observed her sister and appeared sad, holding Michel. Eyes averted, her visage presented an impenetrable wall which discouraged attempts at consolation. Suzanne did not project Fanny's warmth. Florette grabbed my hand and pulled me into her bedroom.

"J'suis contente d'être ici, loin de Papa." (I'm glad to be here, far from Dad.)

"Moi aussi, j'suis bien contente de t'avoir ici." (I'm glad to have you here.)

"You know," Florette continued, "I had to wear the yellow Star of David on my coat when I went outside and in school. I tried to hide it, but it was difficult, and the kids used to call me *sale youpine* (dirty Kike). You are lucky you did not have to wear it!"

"It's scary what you tell me."

"Yes, I know. The worst was when my little Jewish girlfriend's parents were deported. She came to school crying, I did not know how to comfort her and left without seeing Renée again. I wonder what happened."

"Poor girl! We are lucky to be here."

And just like children, during the following summer days, these sad stories were temporarily forgotten. Conspirators in an unfriendly world, we had a close relationship, confiding in each other, sharing fears and sexual questions. The films in Paris, in which the heroine always kissed the hero in the final image, inspired our games. Alternating at being prince charming, we experimented, discovering our bodies. My aristocratic aspirations were reflected in the stories we concocted. Unfortunately, arguments for the role of queen occurred frequently, and compromise was impossible. Maman intervened to protect me, while Tata Fanny defended her daughter. Sometimes an impasse was breeched, with Papa as peacemaker. Unable to remain apart, Florette and I resumed our games until the next disagreement.

Religious schooling was unknown to us. Our schoolmates went to catechism and church. I should have liked to ask for protection from an all-powerful being. Having no god to turn to, Florette and I created our own. It was important, because the Christians around us had one. Our parents never mentioned God; so we fervently prayed (together) to a picture of a white-bearded man cut out from a book of fairy tales. Much later, I discovered with shock that the Jewish religion does not permit a pictorial representation of God and that we had committed a sin. When fear of a Nazi roundup became incessant, Florette and I took comfort in our god (who had Oriental features, now that I think of it). We pasted the image on the wall of Florette's bedroom, above her bed. *Maman would have a fit, had she known!* We prayed before bedtime, whenever I slept in Aunt Fanny's house, awakened early in the morning by Marc, who would jump on our bed, laughing and shaking us. A pillow fight inevitably ensued, and after sending him from the room, we knelt on the bed and prayed, "O God, please save us all from Hitler." The heathen image seemed benevolent and gave us complete confidence!

The war seemed so far away during these warm summer afternoons, when the fields in the back of Florette's house beckoned us to run and play. The tall grass rustled in the soft, breezy afternoon while the cicadas screaked cheerfully as the bees whizzed by, and our only fear was being stung. One day, tired of playing hide-and-seek, we joined other children who were shaking the trees and picking delicious white fleshy cherries called *Bigaros* which had fallen to the ground. Two full huge baskets were gathered. Fanny invited the family to dinner. Dessert consisted of those too abundant, luscious fruit. *Hélas*, I still recall, the belly cramps and trips to the WC during the night, while Maman yelled, *"Oy! Gevalt!* Hitler should feel like this!"

# CHAPTER IX

## YENNE—A PASTORAL LIFE

Yenne, on returning after the war, appeared no different from many French villages. There was the central square, *The Place Centrale*. The church *campanile* (steeple) in the background could be seen not far from the cafés where the men had their *canon* (alcoholic drink) while their wives dutifully went to pray. The town hall, bakery, greengrocer, and other shops all faced the fountain; a relic of former times. The neighboring side streets were narrow, with modest, private homes of sturdy-colored stone construction and wooden shutters which, at once, protect the privacy of their owners while providing a barrier for extremes of temperatures and inclement weather.

The river Rhône flows by the town. Its bridges are destroyed by the retreating French troops, in June 1940. The enemy is able to reach Yenne through the mountain pass (*le Col du Chat*). The German advance is temporarily stopped at Landrecin, a neighboring village, and the force's defensive lines are formed with German and French soldiers, about one hundred meters apart. Due to the overwhelming strength of the Germans, the French forces eventually retreat in disorder, some hiding in farms in the area. The wounded are taken to Dr. Prunier, the local physician. German troops arrive at the gendarmerie in Yenne. One motorcycle with a sidecar contains a bound French officer. The local gendarmes (seven) surrender and are disarmed; their weapons smashed against the wall. Food, especially a most desired item like butter, is requisitioned. This *Petite Victoire* is celebrated with champagne and the bottles then discarded in the empty streets. However, after this night of revelry, the Germans leave the next day to the immense relief of the population. Yenne is apparently not important strategically. (27)

The gendarmerie regains authority under the direction of the Préfecture of Chambéry.

After the war, Yenne looked quaint and charming. The colorful narrow streets were gaily decorated with blooming flowers in many window boxes and in the town's dry fountain. Happy tourists filled the streets and cafés. On the outskirts of the village, modern new homes with flowered little balconies are witness to better times. As a young child, in forced residence, in the winter of 1942, Yenne was gloomy, cold, and damp; the streets seemed huge and forbidding. Lodging was at the local hotel named Labaye (now an old people's home) for a few days, while the rented house was being prepared.

I was immediately enrolled in the intermediary school currently called *Charles Dullin*, after a famous Frenchman (who was born in the neighboring hamlet of Chatelard and founded the Parisian theater *L'Atelier*). Some physical aspects of this school reminded me of Paris. Frosted windows prevented the students from gazing outside. At recess, children played in the inner courtyard. Few trees or flowers were present, and the smell of urine from the latrines permeated the area. The little Parisian girl who came to the country was the antithesis of the *petite paysanne*, with my big bow, pretty dresses, white gloves, and fancy shoes. The girls then would ogle me jealously, and now, as adult women, joke good-naturedly about my *élégance*. The death of the mayor occurred soon after classes began. Presence at the funeral by the student body of the public school was compulsory. The horse-drawn black hearse was followed by the *curé* (priest), choirboys, town officials, and citizenry. Inhaling for the first time a waft of incense, bewildered by it all, I imitated the other "mourners" walking slowly in step to the strains of Chopin's

*Funeral March* played (or more accurately, desecrated) by the local brass band. It was difficult not to laugh at the trombone's explosive sounds, tempered by the noisy flow of the Rhône River alongside the Avenue des Marronniers (chestnut trees). It was a long and boring walk to the cemetery, bounded by stone walls and wrought iron gate. Yennois in their best clothing went there every Sunday after church, and on religious holidays to honor their departed. It was the way of life.

A week after this first civic experience, which also introduced me to Catholicism, the family moved to our furnished new house near the school. The graystone structure and the French windows gave the house a prosperous, bourgeois look. It was in fact a former farmhouse, which was directly entered through the kitchen since it did not have a frontal doorway. The kitchen area was the principal room, the antique black iron stove its main attraction, and also the only source of heat in the house. An adjacent dining-living room with a piano was freezing in the winter, and only inhabited during special occasions. There was a WC on the first floor. Upstairs, one of the two spacious bedrooms, although destined to be mine, was used by Mania. Since fearing to sleep alone, I shared my parents' room, although in a separate bed.

There was a large bathroom on this level. During the week, the family sponge-bathed with heated water. Saturdays were special. The heater could only produce sufficient hot water for one bath. Therefore, each of us took turns in the same bathwater. Papa, as the *Pater Familias*, had the honor of going first. I, Mania, and Maman, in succession, had the dubious distinction to follow, since the water became progressively grayer and colder with each participant's use. Maman could be considered something of a martyr when her turn finally came. This experience was not without some benefit, as we were treated to Father's rather unique renditions of operas initially heard in Germany, but slightly altered. For example, Papa's version of the aria from *Martha* was as follows: "Martha, Martha, du bist schwanger!" A pertinent question came to mind.

"Papa, what does *schwanger* mean?" I asked one day. He laughed.

"Zug gunicht!" (Don't say anything), Maman yelled.

"Why not?" he argued. "It is a normal condition."

"Sie darf dos nit herren" (She should not hear this), was the flat declaration.

Now, really intrigued, I asked, "Papa, what does it mean?"

Maman tried again, "Shah! Shtill, Chaim!" (Keep quiet!) I understood *Chaim*, Father's name in Hebrew.

"Well," Papa said to me, ignoring my mother's glowering expression, "it means pregnant. Martha is expecting a baby." Trying to avoid another one of my embarrassing questions, and glancing uneasily at my mother's back, he added, "C'est une blague!" (It's a joke), just in time as Maman huffed and puffed. Papa chuckled.

The kitchen's window presented a view of passersby, and another large square, the Champ de Foire, which boasted a central, spacious gazebo. Prior to the war, the country fairs regularly took place here. There was a dry water trough used to serve the cattle. The school also faced the Champ de Foire, which was our playground after dismissal. Like Proust's Madeleine, in *A la Recherche du Temps Perdu*, the scent of freshly fallen autumn leaves reminds me now of those playground games from days long ago. The landlord, Monsieur Belon, had a sawmill behind the house, and the loud whining of the machines disturbed the quietude. The felled trees lay strewn on the square, waiting to be hauled away to the mill; but in the interim, became our forts and hills. Florette and I jumped in the crunchy blanket of dry leaves, hiding beneath it or played rough boy's games in order to be accepted by the other children. Florette thought she had a boyfriend, which was a bone of contention. The girls in school ignored us, except for Monsieur Belon's grandchild, Aimée Lenoir, who was our age. Aimée accumulated a pile of her grandfather's wood pieces and sawdust, which were considered treasures. Many of my gifts for Mother's birthdays consisted of oddly shaped wooden fragments, colorfully painted and inscribed with Je t'aime,

Maman! to show my affection. Such games and projects were looked down upon as uninteresting by the older crowd, which included Adrienne, Aimée's sister, fifteen, a pretty, blue-eyed blonde who attracted the boys. Adrienne, who had my complete admiration, was indifferent to us.

I was given a kitten which became my beloved pet. He was a little tiger and was named Pompon. He kept me company while I did my homework, lying quietly on the same table or licking his paws. We were just as inseparable as Florette with Moustique. Pompon began chasing mice as he grew, which was to be expected. Maman's hysterical fear of mice was transmitted to me. When the cat proudly presented a dead mouse hanging from his jaws by the door, Maman promptly climbed on a chair, screaming. I quickly followed while Mania calmly shooed Pompon out. The uncontrolled shrieks abruptly ceased.

The cat was fond of my father. Pompon, who did not like to be ignored, deliberately settled himself on the evening newspaper Papa was reading, noisily purring. After a while, my father attempted to move the cat, but the animal immediately resumed his original position on the paper. Papa gave up with a laugh. Some time later, Pompon became ill, cause unknown. Mania thought he had the flu. Before going to school, I would administer cough syrup with a spoon. He would look at me, and I truly believe, he seemed to be thankful for my attention. On returning from school, one afternoon, Pompon was not there. I was told that he had left and accepted this explanation but was inconsolable for a long time.

Privacy is a very important concept in France. To help assure it, stone walls or high edges surround many homes in countryside villages, while attracting the curiosity of the passersby. On the opposite side of the square lived the aristocrats of the town, an admiral and his brother, a general. Neither the brothers, nor the house, which was well hidden behind a six-foot-high stone wall, were ever seen. To this day their names are unknown to me. Town legend has it that there were well-hidden secrets behind these high walls. For the longest time I thought that monsters or . . . perhaps Germans lurked there. A similar wall faced our house. One day, Madame Lenoir, Aimée's mother, opened the wooden gate. I fully anticipated the Big Bad Wolf but hoping for Madame de Ségur's fairyland! Instead, there was only a vegetable garden! What a disappointment! Also, what a relief; no monsters, no Germans!

Papa was very interested in this garden and decided to develop one of his own now that he was a country dweller. Monsieur Belon, who liked Papa, lent him a narrow section of land, and my father proceeded to plant potatoes and carrots, which the rabbits promptly devoured. Papa was determined however and put up fences to no avail. The rabbits were just as persistent, especially with the carrots. The potatoes grew, but their leaves were attacked by a bug, the *doriphore*. Mania and I awakened early with sunrise to remove them. It didn't help. The leaves were destroyed. My father finally gave up.

Maman was more successful in her endeavors; she had four egg-laying chickens and two geese who gracefully toddled along in the street with ribbons around their necks. They became our pets. So did the chickens. They all had names, now forgotten, except for *La Belle* and *La Patronne*, who seemed indeed to boss the others, including the rooster.

Mania was responsible for food supplies and perceived as the manager of the household, while Maman played the lady of the manor, always the elegant *grande dame*. People from Traize, a village in the mountains, and of Yenne, still remember Mania, accompanied by my aunt Fanny, making friends with the farmers or *paysans*. They recalled her old cotton dress covered by a flowery apron over multiple layers of clothing. Socks were rolled up or down on top of the wooden shoes or slippers, depending on the weather. A drab sweater hanging limply on her shoulders, she carried an eternal *cabas* (shopping bag) made of brown sturdy cloth, which was, often successfully, filled with produce.

"Alors, qu'est-ce que vous avez pour moi?" (So, what have you got for me?) would be her introductory remark. These friendly contacts became very useful later on, when "safe houses" were needed. Old shoes were traded for milk, butter, and flour, when these staples came in short supply. Food in the country was not as scarce as in the cities. The black market flourished. Once, Mania brought back one hundred kilos of flour which Madame Lenoir saved in the attic. To express our appreciation, she was invited to the house to sample Maman's *blintzes* (crepes filled with white cheese). Unfortunately, they did not appeal to her, which was discovered many years later.

Papa, when cash was needed, sometimes brought gold coins to Monsieur Chagnon, who had a contact in Chambéry, and who in turn carried out the exchange in a bank, since there was none in Yenne. Occasionally, Papa reluctantly went to exchange *Harte* (gold Louis) or *Lokschen* (dollars) himself. It was dangerous because the Préfecture in Chambéry knew of our residence. Should the authorities check documents, Papa could be apprehended. Often, Fanny would carry out these transactions as she and her family, having voluntarily joined us in Yenne, were not registered in Chambéry. Madame Thévenard, whose husband was a gendarme, gave Fanny her identity card for the day's trip, a total distance of fifty kilometers by bicycle.

Madame Lenoir taught Maman and Fanny to make soap and jam for which Maman bought a huge copper tub. It was a big production. The tub was set on the shiny cast iron stove/oven. It was hot in the kitchen. Maman and Mania, a reluctant helper, perspired heavily while mixing the ingredients with great determination. Jam smelled sweet, but the odor of soap-making was unpleasant.

Maman baked bread once a week. It was a sort of *brioche*. The inviting aroma would extend to the street and greet me on returning from school. The house smelled warm and welcoming. Maman had to play the martyr once again and dramatically reminded Papa how hard she was working. Tobacco was scarce, and Papa saved his cigarette butts. As soon as Maman whined, I watched as my father silently emptied the tobacco from his *mégots* on a small paper, carefully rolled it, licking the paper before gently pressing it, lit the cigarette with a match, and pensively smoked. The whole routine seemed to calm him. While jealous of each other, Mania and Maman stood by the burning stove, bickering like two angry hens. It was exasperating!

So many of my friends who spent the war years in Paris or other large cities complained about the scarcity of food. Many villagers, including the Jewish families, certainly did not suffer in this regard.

However, not everyone there was so fortunate. Yenne was near the Italian border. Italians who were starving in their own country would come to work in France, especially from the city of Modane, but did not fare any better in this small town. One woman, in particular, attracted the attention of my mother and, having no husband, tried to find a job as a domestic. Maman felt great sympathy for her and provided some domestic work which was really not needed, as well as food for the family. In the winter, the poor, coatless woman wore a thin dress and slippers. Her six children would pass the house on their way to school, also scantily dressed, often without shoes, sometimes with filthy, scabby knees and nonhealing sores. This sight was extremely disturbing for Maman, and they were given warm clothing and footwear.

Eventually, there were approximately one hundred Jewish families settled in Yenne, of whom we knew relatively few. On my third trip to the town in 1989, I met a Yennoise named Odile and was surprised to discover that her family had lodged about forty Jews during the war, in their *pension* (boarding house). She recalled being regarded as a sister by one of the tenants and was presented with a manicure set for her twentieth birthday in 1944. Samuel, another lodger, was one of three brothers who had left their wives in Paris and lived in Yenne (*I wondered why, but never inquired*). His brother Paul, an extremely fat man, would read the newspaper while floating down the Rhône. Pierre, Odile's husband, returned to Paris one day and found red crosses on their respective apartment doors indicating that the wives had been deported. A Madame Cohen lived at the *pension* with her daughter and grandchild. Max Ochsman rented a room too, with his mistress, who would periodically go to Paris to obtain funds from his son-in-law, Claude. They were never invited to the house.

The Mirrelwassers and their teenage daughter were, at first, simply acquaintances. The Zalmans became our friends because their daughter, Sylvie, was my age. Since there was no radio available, entertainment consisted primarily of socializing with other Jewish families. Maman baked a specialty of the region called *gâteau de Savoie*, a sort of very light sponge cake, and served it with tea in glasses, which was sipped slowly while sucking on a piece of sugar *à la Russe*. An added treat was my balletic interpretation of the *Liszt's Rhapsody*, learned at the Studio Wacker, accompanied by Maman's lyrical rendition. This was particularly enjoyed by Mr. Zalman, who applauded enthusiastically at the end of the performance, calling me a *scheyne meidele* (a pretty little girl). Dancing continued to be a joy.

Since there was a piano, Maman "insisted" that lessons resume with Madame Dupont, who resided on the Place Centrale. She was in her seventies, usually clad in a long dark dress, with a tight black velvet ribbon around her neck; she would tug the loose skin hanging beneath her chin, as she listened to me perform. Although crippled by arthritis, Madame managed to play beautifully. Florette also studied with her. One day, on returning alone from the class, a few boys followed me, jeering: "Eh! La Fernande, la youpine!" I walked faster as they approached and began throwing stones, laughing and yelling: "sale youpine!" (dirty kike). No one came to the rescue. Scared out of my wits, I took off at full speed, holding the music tightly, tears running down my face. Although the piano lessons continued (Madame Dupont was a favorite), I never again went to her house alone. Madame was impressed by my heartfelt interpretation of *Tristesse* by Chopin. This sheet music with a written dedication after the war still remains in my possession.

Although Madame Dupont is remembered with affection, the piano, ah! the piano . . . however, was a struggle. I disliked studying, and Maman forced me to practice half an hour every day. Of course this became another source of conflict. One evening, she ordered me to play for our guests, without prior mention, presupposing a negative response. She was correct. I refused anyway, fearful of making mistakes, but more importantly, of placing my bitten fingernails and swollen, bleeding cuticles within easy view. Monsieur Zalman kindly did not insist and diplomatically directed the activity towards belote, a favorite pastime. Papa understood and started the card game immediately. My loud sigh of relief was noted by Monsieur Zalman, who smiled knowingly. This pleasant evening was short lived. My father and Mania were partners. Papa who appreciated a good joke, tried to cheat by telling Mania that the windows needed to be washed (*carreaux* in French can mean windows or diamonds) Mania either did not comprehend or ignored this obvious signal. The Zalmans also did not appear to notice, so absorbed were they in the game. They lost. Sylvie and I looked at each other. "You know," she whispered, "it probably means we won't see you for a while."

They left soon after. Sylvie was correct in her prediction. However, the families were very close in those days. And after a time, the visits were resumed.

There were also some unmarried Jews in Yenne. Maman felt morally obligated to take lonely folks under a protective wing and also desiring to find a *shidech* (arranged marriage) for Mania, a practical and socially accepted method of removing her from the household. There was one man in particular nicknamed *Der Speier* (the Spitter) by my mother. His wife and two children had been deported. He had escaped capture, having been on a business trip. For a long time, I thought *Der Speier* was his true name. He was tall and skinny, usually dressed in black, wearing a dirty shirt. The moment he seated himself at the kitchen table to sip *tchai* and eat a *kichel*, the latest news would be related. The fingers of his right hand tapped a rhythmic staccato on the kitchen table, which vaguely sounded like Bizet's *William Tell Ouverture*, while his eyelids blinked rapidly in synchrony. Those present carefully chose to remain at a distance in order to avoid being struck by profuse droplets of spittle; as he spoke too quickly. Thus, the surname, "The Spitter." This proved just too tempting since I mean-mindedly caricatured this poor man after a visit. My antics again caused Maman to refer to me as a *schlang* (snake), nevertheless, with a slight smirk on her face. Alas, the romance with Mania never materialized since she was too busy scrounging for food and arguing with my mother. Most sadly, *Der Speier* was later arrested in a raid in Chambéry and was never seen again.

# CHAPTER X

## A LESSON IN TOLERANCE

The image of the French word *Juif* remains vivid. It was printed in large red letters in my parents' identity card and on the six-pointed yellow star worn on outer garments. Huge propaganda posters in the métro depicted Jews as greedy, sneering, and filthy, with the usual hooked nose . . . and labeled prominently: JUIF. As a youth, I never admitted my Jewish origins, being either afraid or ashamed to do so. Today, while proud of my heritage, I still experience anxiety when this subject is raised, recalling malicious comments such as, "Still waiting for the Messiah?" or "sale youpine!" (dirty kike). Paradoxically, both the Star of David and the swastika put me ill at ease, despite the exhilaration I feel on viewing the beautiful blue-and-white flag of Israël. With the return of worldwide anti-Semitism, particularly in Europe and especially in France, this anxiety does not diminish.

American Jews who use the pejorative Yiddish term *Schwarze*, which literally means "black," when referring to African Americans upset me. Neither can I abide other ethnic or racial slurs, too reminiscent of the disparaging phrases endured during my family's Forced Residence in Yenne. It was demeaning and humiliating. I felt like a despicable nonperson, and my self-esteem was nonexistent.

I have heard it said that "in every warm Christian heart there is a cold spot for the Jews." Yet, in my view, Jews themselves should reflect most carefully on this issue. Tolerance, regardless of race, religion, or ethnic origin, must be taught in the home, instead of bigotry and hatred, and strongly reinforced in the school experience. My family and many other Jews were saved by honorable, decent, and courageous Christians who felt very strongly about the injustice and cruelty of the Nazi regime and placed themselves at great risk in doing so.

I shall never forget Madame Moliaix.

Her title in France was *institutrice*, to be distinguished from *professeur*. This latter designation is given only to the elite educators who have studied in the hallowed halls of the *Ecole Normale Supérieure* and later qualify to teach at the *Lycée* or academic high school. Some renowned French intellectuals have taught at the *Lycée* such as Georges Pompidou and Jean-Paul Sartre. There was no *Lycée* in Yenne, only a *Cours Complémentaire* (lower secondary school) which followed the primary school.

It should be understood that the French school system had undergone profound changes since its great reform in 1870. In 1917, a group of professors were incorporated and created a movement to unify the French educational system and make it more democratic. Some principles were made into law. The *Lycée*, one of Napoléon I's many famous institutions, was costly for the average French family and therefore, benefited the wealthy until the early 1930s. Most children would attend primary and middle schools until the age of thirteen and obtain a *Certificat d'Etudes* for graduation. In 1924, teachers unionized, and from 1930 to 1933, no tuition was required at the *Lycée* for academically capable students. (Currently, public education including the *Lycée* is free.) Strikes to improve the teachers' working conditions ensued in 1934 and 1938 but were unsuccessful. The unions tended to be socialistic, supportive of the Popular Front and of peace. Later, this antagonized Pétain and other collaborators who thought that socialism was at the root of France's problems. Liberal republicanism, including the reformed educational system, was not in Vichy's political agenda, and so a return to the "old" primary and secondary school systems took place. (28)

Madame Moliaix was a product of the "old" system, sharing the education of the villagers' children with her husband. They had a boy and a girl who attended a boarding school in Chambéry in order to receive an academic *Lycée* education, which led to the university and greater professional opportunities. The Moliaix family lived in a house adjoining the school, but their privacy was well protected by a courtyard enclosed by an iron fence. They did not socialize with the local townspeople.

Madame Moliaix, who taught French, was the artist of the family. The walls of our class were decorated with her gentle water color canvases of flowers which introduced the art of drawing and painting to the students. Madame Moliaix also had practical skills. The girls learned sewing, embroidery, knitting, crochet, and the long-lost craft of darning torn socks. No materials were wasted during the war. Blankets made of knitted woolen squares sewn together were sent to the prisoners of war. Popular tunes such as *Une Fleur au Chapeau* and *Mon Vieux Chalet* were taught in schools because the Petainist government thought the lyrics encouraged the virtues of honesty and patriotism.

French grammar was puzzling for me, but eventually, it was mastered after frequent dictations. Compositions, which could be so boring, were rendered interesting by Madame Moliaix, who would share worthwhile literary student efforts. I took great pride on hearing my "misadventure" at the Demarcation Line being read to the class. A foreign language was required in the curriculum. Madame Moliaix taught Italian but was not adverse to my learning English instead. It seemed relevant to study English at the age of ten in 1942, in order to properly greet the Allied troops, should they ever pass through the village. The young wife of the local land surveyor was found to acquaint Papa and me with the mysteries of this language. The lessons were very amusing because Papa had difficulty pronouncing the English *th* sound, jokingly stating that a pencil between the teeth or a hot potato was needed to enunciate it correctly. However, learning that *Jane is a girl* and that *Jack is a boy* did not help very much when listening to Winston Churchill on BBC Radio-

London. Not a word was understood. Papa, in order to hide his own ignorance, would yell, *"Quoi?"* (What?) All this money was spent, and you don't understand Churchill!" Although even greater effort was made, it was to no avail, since my teacher had a very marked French accent, and Churchill's speech was heavily accented as well, and garbled at best.

In 1985, after working for over fifteen years at a girls' Catholic high school, the Academy of the Holy Angels, in northern New Jersey, Sr. Ann, the new principal, asked me to offer the opening prayer for the next faculty meeting.

"Sister, I am Jewish, you know."

"That's all right, we have the same God, unless you prefer not to do it," she replied without hesitation and with a smile which was returned. With some trepidation, I accepted. *What would I do?* This faculty meeting was to take place just before Rosh Hashanah, the Jewish New Year of which I knew little. The religion faculty was far more knowledgeable, and I therefore decided to relate an incident that occurred at school during the war.

On that day, Florette and I are seated in adjoining seats, listening to Madame Moliaix's grammar lesson. Deeply attentive, I almost fail to notice a white-faced Florette's trembling hand as she passes along a note. The paper crudely depicts a familiar face with hooked nose and chin, and horns, entitled: "JUIF SUSS" with signatures of the students. Madame Moliaix walks through the class, oblivious to the drama until she stops by our desk. Noticing the silent exchange between Florette and me, she interrupts the lecture and says, "Qu'est-ce qu'il y a?" (What's the matter?) Angrily, I thrust the paper forward. After glancing at it briefly, she tears it in pieces. Madame Moliaix is a tall, thin woman. Her obvious distress is betrayed by flushed cheeks and protruding veins on temples and neck. Glaring at the class, she proceeds to talk about the difficult times, tolerance, accepting people who are different from ourselves, and finally asks the group to apologize. Not a sound is heard. The moment is tense. Florette and I hold hands. I am cold, my throat is tight, and my eyes strangely full. The class, without great enthusiasm, responds to Madame Moliaix's command and a chorus of "Pardon, Fernande *et* Florette" breaks the total silence.

During the faculty meeting at Holy Angels, so many years later, my colleagues listened attentively to my story, also in that absolute silence. I concluded, " . . . and so my friends, I feel vindicated today, being able to tell this story without fear, to Christians in a Catholic school in the United States. I wish my fellow students could see me. Since this meeting is taking place before Rosh Hashanah, it is customary to inscribe family and friends in the Book of Life, and this is what I am doing today. *Le shanah tovah tikka tevu.*" Everyone responded with "Amen," some with tears in their eyes, as I was feeling great exhilaration that the pariah could speak of this matter to the group, finally without fear.

*Hélas*, at that time, although my fellow students had apologized, it had been but lip service. Their taunts continued. Madame Moliaix had to intervene in many fights in the following years. The village people were either pro-Vichy or procommunist. The wise ones kept silent, awaiting the final victor. To be addressed as a "dirty Red" was as insulting as "dirty Kike." Frankly, I did not know what a "Red" was but nevertheless understood it was an insult. The son of the hardware store owner, a good-looking tall boy on whom I had a crush, harassed me on the playground. Although small in stature, I could not abide his insults and one day (*to hell with his good looks*) promptly kicked him in the shins, calling him "dirty Red."

Another nemesis was the same girl who inspired the class with the drawn caricature of the *Juif Süss*, with whom, oddly, I also wished to be friendly, but to no avail. She continued calling me nasty names. Finally one day, I grabbed her hair, slapped her, and yelled: "Dirty Red!"

"I am not a dirty Red!"

"Yes, you are. Let's go see Madame Moliaix." With a determined step and without looking at each other, we marched to Madame Moliaix's house. She opened the door smiling and was immediately bombarded by our recriminations: "She calls me a dirty Red," the girl shouted.

"She called me a dirty Kike," I yelled back.

"You can't talk to each other this way, children. You don't even understand what you are saying. Be good girls and apologize to each other. Remember what I said the other day about tolerance. Come on, make up and *embrassez-vous!*" It felt like the kiss of death. The girl and I reluctantly obeyed and left, both very dissatisfied with the verdict. I really had thought Madame Moliaix would support me but later realized that, as our teacher, she needed to be evenhanded.

Her wisdom and courage were inspiring. She was greatly respected by Maman and was blessed at every opportunity with, "Soll zey sine gesind." Once, while bicycling at high speed and without control, I fell, severely lacerating my knee, which required a week's bed rest. Great! No school! Reading all day long and being served meals in bed! What luxury! However, Madame Moliaix's weekly recounting of *Mathias Sandorf* by Jules Verne, a story of adventure and revenge, was greatly missed. Poor Mother was a slave, responding to the slightest beck and call, briefly interrupted, one afternoon, by Madame Moliaix's visit to determine the cause of my absence. Maman took the opportunity to speak of the war and fears for my safety.

"I want to thank you for what you did the other day with the *Juif Süss* incident," she said, in her broken French.

"C'était tout à fait normal." Madame Moliaix did not hesitate.

"It was not such a normal reaction, Madame," said Maman tearfully. "It was very brave during this dangerous period. What is to be done if there is a raid and Fernande and Florette are in school?"

"Don't worry, Madame Henri, Monsieur Moliaix and I, we'll hide the children in the closets if need be."

She took my mother's hands in her own and smiled reassuringly. Watching this exchange with glee, I took advantage of my teacher's encouraging and benevolent attitude and asked Madame Moliaix if she would lend me *Mathias Sandorf.*

"I am sorry, Fernande," she says, chuckling, "but you have to come to school and listen with the others. It would not be fair to them." *How disappointing.* Slyly, I asked Papa to purchase the book when in Chambéry.

Madame Moliaix was unaware that the story was prematurely finished. It did not matter. Her readings continued and were pure pleasure. Each character was portrayed, which made the story so interesting and alive. This book, in the green edition of *La Bibliothèque Verte*, remains in my library. The cover is a bit torn, and the pages slightly yellow. Jules Verne's *Mathias Sandorf* resembles Alexandre Dumas' *Le Comte de Monte Cristo*. Both main characters, betrayed by enemies, seek revenge. Analogously, the Nazis and Vichy were the enemies. Free France's revenge was awaited. Perhaps this was the intent that Madame Moliaix wished to convey in choosing this story. It was very relevant, at least for me.

Monsieur Moliaix taught history, geography, geology, chemistry, physics, and arithmetic. He was also a formidable character. A wiry man in his forties, who taught with a stentorious voice and sparse gestures, he terrorized everyone. His desk was on a foot-high platform. When the boys were unable to answer a question, the pupils watched with dread as he silently and slowly descended, glaring at the culprit, long ruler in hand and, upon reaching his victim, slammed the ruler on the head. The girls were never touched physically but rather verbally insulted with pejoratives such as, "Espèce d'oie," "Espèce de crétine," "Espèce d'idiote," "Espèce de buse" (specimen of goose, cretin, nitwit, buzzard). Feeling unworthy and humiliated, no one dared utter a sound.

Arithmetic was a subject extremely difficult for me (and also for Papa, who tried to help). Problems involved the speed of trains approaching each other and of water dripping from faucets! *Who cared!* Hours were spent in trying to solve them. Finally, Papa would guess at the solution or use (his) algebra, which was foreign to me, at the time.

"Ça y est, j'ai trouvé" (That's it, I found the solution), Papa would exclaim triumphantly.

"Comment tu as fait?" (How did you do it?), I would ask with wonder.

"Je n'sais pas, mais c'est comme ça!" (I don't know, but that's how it is!) He seemed so certain.

"Ah! bon!" (Oh! OK!) I would shrug and accept his solution.

I tearfully returned home with a failing grade. Papa, remorseful and consoling, would promise to do better! After continued failures, I struggled with the trains and faucets myself, risking Monsieur Moliaix's verbal abuse.

Chemistry lessons were equally frightening. Florette and I, desk near "the platform," worriedly exchanged glances, ready to escape the inevitable small explosion resulting from Monsieur Moliaix's experiments with volatile gases.

The geography lesson concerning Egypt is forever engraved in memory. Monsieur Moliaix queried, "What monument reminds us of a geometric form?" Knowing the answer, I was impatient to respond but became confused as my hand shot up in the air, and I yelled, "C'est le Pharynx!"

"Non, non," shouted Florette, raising her hand, "c'est le Larynx!"

"Idiotes!" chuckled Monsieur Moliaix. "It's not the pharynx or the larynx!"

"I know, I know," wanting to salvage the situation, "c'est le Lynx!"

"Espèce de buses! Espèce de crétines!" He burst out laughing. "You mean the Sphinx! And the monument is the Pyramid."

The Moliaixes were implacable when it came to cleanliness. A farm boy, Jean Meunier, from a family of fourteen brothers and sisters, was lice ridden, along with others in the class. Thorough weekly inspections were carried out by the Moliaix. The lice-carrying victim's hair was cut, shaved, and shampooed. Once again, no one had the temerity to complain, particularly Jean, who never studied the lessons, and whose head continually was at the punitive end of Monsieur Moliaix's ruler. The couple's method of education was old-fashioned, primitive perhaps, and not acceptable by modern educational standards, but effective. Madame Moliaix played the good guy and he, the bad. Both made school an enjoyable experience, at least for me. She tried to protect us from the hostility and cruelty of the other children.

Madame Moliaix was exceptional and served as my inspiration years later, as an educator myself, with particular regard to confronting prejudice and intolerance.

# CHAPTER XI

## THE COURAGE OF FEW

The Vichy government of collaboration initially attempted to send volunteer workers to Germany in September 1942, but without great success. It then decided that men, eighteen to fifty years old, and single women, twenty-one to thirty-five years of age, were subject to any work judged useful to the Third Reich. Pierre Laval aided the Nazi *Organization Todt*, which recruited people from the occupied nations for work camps in Germany or to construct the defensive wall along the Atlantic coast of France. He established the SOT (*Service Obligatoire du Travail*) with the *Relève* System: for every three skilled workers sent to Germany, one French prisoner of war (of which there were two million) would be released. The program was mandatory. (29) The young *paysans* and villagers from Yenne tried to avoid this order, by hiding in the mountains or joining the Résistance (*Maquis*). Others, like André Chagnon, who worked for his father, prepared for the eventuality of a Vichy-inspired civilian roundup.

There was a stream behind the Chagnon's house in which André placed a chair and rubber boots, also attaching a strong rope from the small balcony overlooking the stream. His parents would divert the searching gendarmes' attention in pleasant conversation, while André slipped down the rope, put on the boots, and sat in the water throughout the day and night. The police knew of the subterfuge and turned a blind eye, but

Chambéry did not. One day Monsieur Chagnon Père was taken hostage to the city and would have been imprisoned, unless André registered for the SOT. Fortunately, André had a friend in the higher echelons of the Préfecture who falsified his documents. André found himself suddenly "married, with a child," and so, was excused from the *Relève* program. As time went by however, unable to sustain the deception any longer, he departed to the mountains to join the *Maquis*.

Those of us in *Résidance Forcée* were very vulnerable. The Nazis and their Vichy collaborators knew our exact whereabouts. The French Milice, which was created in 1943 by Vichy as a fascist police force, would visit Yenne periodically, to find those registered nonworkers. A representative of the Todt Organization who was headquartered in the village would also carry out similar surveys. The Jews in the village attempted to find jobs even as volunteers, in order to escape the labor camps, but unaware that they could be deported anyway.

Papa worked in the farm fields for our friends, the Thomases, who had a grocery on the Place Centrale. The physical labor was extremely demanding, and Papa was not accustomed to it, having worked primarily as an administrator in the shoe factory for many years. Bouts of arthritis only added to the difficulty. He also helped with the weaving of wicker baskets, sometimes sleeping in a storage room on the second floor above the grocery store. However, a certificate now attested that he was working, albeit without monetary compensation. In Lyon and Grenoble, raids were successfully capturing Jews, regardless of work status, for labor and concentration camps.

Former government officials such as Blum, Gamelin (30), Jouhaud (31), and Daladier (32) were transported to Germany. Darnand (33) became an SS officer, and Doriot (34) received the Iron Cross, for services rendered. He later was assassinated by the *Maquis*. Général de Lattre de Tassigny, who had been condemned to a ten-year prison term, escaped to North Africa. (35) This news came via the gendarmerie, the local police station. The *Capitaine de Gendarmerie*, Langlois, thought that Pétain and

Laval were to be greatly admired and praised! Biking by our house, the *capitaine* would sometimes stop and flirt with Mania, bragging about the government and his own "important" role. Mania was generally teased because of this powerful "boyfriend." Indeed, the *capitaine* apparently liked Mania, who played along, smiling, gold tooth glistening, as she attentively listened to his comments (never contradicting him), nodding her head approvingly. Mania and Maman, later in the evening, conjointly came forth with the same oft-repeated curse, "Soll er gehn in drerd!" Maman thought Mania had some influence with him.

One day, Maman needed a permit to visit a physician in Aix-Les-Bains. Resolutely, we strode to the gendarmerie, she *ferputzt* (all dressed up) in her finest dress and fur coat, with stained, stocking-colored legs and a false seam, leather gloves, and purse. *Capitaine* Langlois, already rotund, chest expanded to appear more impressive, neglected to offer my mother a chair but said, rather in a sneering and sugary tone, "Vous n'avez pas besoin de docteur, Madame Henri, vous avez bonne mine!" (You don't need a doctor, Madame Henri, you look well!), as we stood before his desk. Indeed, Maman appeared healthy with her

Yenne—Our house, nowadays

Yenne—The Moliaix's house

hennaed pompadour and rouged cheeks. Little did he know (or care) that she suffered from kidney stones and high blood pressure! Maman responded with her most charming smile, whose underlying meaning and unstated curse I intuitively appreciated, but fortunately, he didn't. Langlois finally granted the pass, like a lord bestowing a boon to a serf, after asking many superfluous questions.

Thankfully, there was a young gendarme named Arsène Thévenard. Maman and his wife Jeanne became acquainted, as the young woman passed our house one day with her baby, whom Maman admired. Eventually, Maman told her of the potential danger faced by our family and other Jews. As a result, Arsène, on learning at the gendarmerie of prospective raids by the milice (36) would so inform Jeanne. She, in turn, then came to warn us, whatever the time of day or weather conditions. Papa, then traveling by bike, sounded the alarm (like Paul Revere) among the Jewish community, who then packed clothing and food and temporarily took refuge in the mountains. Sometimes there was great urgency. On such an occasion, the family was lunching at Tata Fanny's. It was winter, snow was falling. Jeanne, wearing slippers and a thin sweater, rushed in the house, short of breath;

she had obviously been running and directly urged, "Partez immediatement, et cachez-vous!" (Leave immediately and hide!) The milice had stopped their vehicle at the gendarmerie and were seeking the locations of the Jews. She was certain that Langlois would cooperate. Leaving the food on the table, grabbing warm clothes and boots, we ran through the fields into the woods, well beyond the house. Initially, it was an adventure for the children who were giggling, playing hide-and-seek, and throwing snowballs. We became quickly subdued by the worried facial expressions of our parents and were bidden to hide quietly in the forest, which was difficult since we were shivering from the cold. After several hours, Papa went to investigate and decided it was safe to return to the house.

During my visit to Yenne in 2000, I spoke to Jeanne Thévenard, now residing near Dijon, by telephone. Bless her heart. My parents were still quite vivid in her memory, although I was not. She was now a very old widowed lady, with an adult son. I'll never forget her sweet, gentle face framed by curly long light-blond hair and laughing blue eyes.

However, in early spring, because of the potential danger, and at Maman's insistence, it was decided to leave Yenne for a brief period. Unbelievably, it was not considered necessary for Tata Fanny's family to come along since there was no man eligible for the SOT who could be threatened with transportation to Germany. Under the circumstances, this was a clear misperception of the facts, since Jews were being regularly deported to the camps by the milice. Mania, nevertheless, remained to keep tabs on the house and warn us, if necessary, feeling certain of her own safety, while possibly obtaining additional information from Capitaine Langlois.

I cannot remember with absolute certainty to which mountain village we fled during this period. It was either Traize or St-Jean-deChevelu, but probably the former since André Chagnon indicated that a trading relationship had been established with the farmers of Traize, exchanging food for money and shoes. Years later, both were visited: quiet small villages, ghostlike, with some stray chickens on the town square, a few houses, and no visible inhabitants. Perhaps they were working in the fields? In any case, there was no one to interview, and we returned disappointed to Yenne.

The dash to the mountains takes place in the late evening. The bus brings us to a farm. There is total darkness. The accommodations have not yet been prepared. The night is spent in the main house. Papa sleeps on the kitchen floor, covered with blankets. Maman and I have a room with an iron bed, which does not look inviting. The sheets are gray and dirty, causing us to shudder, so we stretch out on top of the blanket, fully clothed, warmed by Maman's fur coat. It is cold in the room. Maman snuggles up against me, spoon-fashion, and sleep soon comes. The following day, we settle in the neighboring barn. It is a large room with basic furniture, combining sleeping and living quarters. meals consist of simple farm fare: soup, bread, and cheese. Dinner is shared in the main house. The chant of the rooster, cackling of the chickens, and the delicious aroma of fresh-baked bread awaken us in the early morning. Breakfast is a special treat which includes dunking thick slices of homemade wheat bread, dripping in butter, in a big bowl of café au lait. The smell of strongly brewed French coffee still conjures up these images. With an eye to my health, Maman insists on another dietary torture, namely drinking milk straight from the cow. The nauseating taste and odor of the steaming raw white liquid makes me retch and spit it out. Maman yells: "Why?" I run to the house without responding.

My parents are delighted to find that the Mirrelwassers are in a neighboring farm. Days are spent with little to do except observe Papa and Mr. Mirrelwasser playing belote or chess for hours on end. I learn both games but later develop an aversion to playing cards; it is too reminiscent of this period.

Maman has made a small red blouse which is not to be worn near the bull. Occasionally, the farmer's wife requests that I watch the cows or pick dandelions for salad. Ignoring the warning while in the field, the bull spots the crimson cloth and dashes directly toward me. Sheepish and frightened, I barely make it over the fence but definitely do not want to return home and face disapproval or possible punishment. It is sunny, a light breeze caresses my cheek. Enough of belote, chess, and knitting! *Vive la joie*, running free on the mountain, far from the bull, the cows, and my parents!

*Pissenlits* (dandelions) are picked (for the salad), and daffodils are very proudly presented to the farmer's wife. She smiles and says: "Alors, as-tu bien gardé les animaux?" (So, were you a good shepherdess?)

"Mais bien sûr!" (But of course!) Proud of myself, I have arrived just in time for Maman's preparation of the evening meal consisting of preferred Russian delicacies: dandelion salad, marinated herring, borscht, and boiled potatoes, not my favorites. I grimace. The farmer, however, finds the dishes delectable and, to our dismay, shows his appreciation by pouring wine in the beet soup and mixing the concoction with his knife!

Sitting around the table and sipping tea after supper, I find it soothing to observe the farmer's wife spinning wool by the soft glow of an oil lamp. The wool is rough to the touch, but I imagine warm, knitted socks for Papa. The farmer adds some wood to the stove, and a warm, homey feeling permeates the room, as the whirring sound of the spinning wheel lulls me peacefully to sleep. The following day Maman is persuaded to buy some wool and is taught to knit socks. I make the top, heel, and toes, and Maman knits the remaining space between. It is very efficient. The socks are indestructible and, in fact, last for years.

Not all memories are as tranquil. Shouting and frantically clucking chickens are heard in the yard, one afternoon. Curious, I step through the door to investigate and abruptly stop, fascinated by a most obscene spectacle: a chicken without a head running around the yard, chased by the farmer's wife who finally catches it. Lunch is promptly regurgitated. Maman rushes to my rescue. Needless to mention that this chicken is not eaten. Perhaps it is hypocritical. Although eating poultry is rather enjoyable, I have absolutely no desire to know the precise method of its demise. This is also true of killed rabbits which are usually skinned and hung in the barn to season, visible to all. For this reason, I cannot abide eating rabbits. Country life definitely does not appeal to me. Contact with civilization thankfully comes via the farmer's radio.

Occasionally, Maman sings along with a vocalist on a musical program: "J'attendrai, le jour et la nuit." (I'll wait, night and day.) "J'attendrai toujours, ton retour." (I'll wait for your return.)

This song has particular meaning for those who have loved ones detained somewhere in Germany.

Broadcasts from London are also heard surreptitiously, introduced by the famous first four notes of Beethoven's *Fifth Symphony* and followed by the phrase: "Les Français parlent aux Français" (The French speak to the French). The listeners are warned to distrust Radio-Paris. Amusing lyrics to the popular tune of "La Kukaratcha" are heard as follows: "Radio-Paris *ment.*" (Radio-Paris lies.)

"Radio-Paris *ment.*" (Radio-Paris lies.)

"Radio-Paris *est allemand.*" (Radio-Paris is German.)

There are coded messages such as "Les poules ont pondu leurs oeufs" (the chickens have laid their eggs). Could it be the invasion or a bombardment? Churchill provides another brief address, and Papa is convinced that I shall never master English. Although listening with intense concentration, I find his words still largely incomprehensible and frustrating. It was enriching and delightful after becoming truly bilingual in adulthood to finally appreciate Churchill's uplifting speeches and oratorical skills.

Return to Yenne occurs several weeks later, after receiving a message from Mania stating that it is safe.

With a few exceptions, there was no love lost between the *paysans* and the Jews. They harbored us and were well paid. They also sold produce at black market prices. The French government devaluated the franc in the 1950s, requesting its citizenry to bring in "old money" in exchange for the new bills. It was not surprising when the *paysans* came to the banks with huge *lessiveuses* (laundry vats) filled with paper currency. (37)

Still ignored or insulted by other children, Florette and I

continue as playmates, sometimes joined by my neighbor Aimée
Lenoir or Sylvie Zalman. Initially, Sylvie and I share both mutual
admiration and envy. Sylvie is tall and slim, blond and blue eyed,
while in sharp contrast, I am a small brunette.

"I have ballerina's legs," she proudly announces one day,
extending skinny limbs for view. (*My legs are plump.*)

"Do you know what are 'Lokschen and Harte'?" I counter,
with a smug smile. *Ha! Ha! I've got her.* Happily, she looks
confused.

"No, what is it?" she answers, forgetting her legs for the
moment. (*I still wish those legs were mine!*)

"Well, I can't tell you, my parents say you can't talk about
that. The walls have ears."

"So why did you bring it up? What is it?" Her curiosity is
piqued.

"I can't tell you, ask your parents!" Frustrated, she angrily
leaves. I never told anyone else either.

(*I almost knew how to keep a secret.*)

Sylvie's parents continued to visit occasionally. News obtained
from the BBC or the gendarmerie's dispatches were discussed.
Hopes arose with reports that the Free French were well
established in the colonies of Martinique, Guadeloupe, and Algier
had rallied in support of de Gaulle. Marseille, on the other hand,
was the site of numerous Jewish arrests. The Demarcation Line
had disappeared, and Germans invaded the Free Zone in 1943,
even replacing the Italians in Cannes, because their
administration was considered insufficiently harsh! The Italians
and Hitler were usually the targets of Mr. Zalman's jokes to my
mother's delight.

Monsieur Zalman is sitting at a café on Place Centrale, in the
summer of 1943; his wife, mother-in-law, and daughter Sylvie,
severely ill with pneumonia, at home. Two militiamen, who have
parked their truck in front of the bakery, enter the store,
apparently to locate Jews. Monsieur Zalman observes the situation
at the bakery, panics, and runs out on the street. The militiamen,
supposing that he is Jewish, pursue and pistol-whip him. Monsieur

Zalman frantically defends himself but is overcome, dragged to the truck, and driven away. The baker had witnessed the events and, relating them fifty-six years later, admitted that he wanted to stop the beating but was prevented from doing so by his wife. Fear of reprisal was rampant. In a small village like Yenne, the news of this event spreads like wildfire! Someone hurries to warn Madame Zalman, who places her mother, sick daughter, and a few belongings in a neighbor's car and flees to the protection of a convent. Madame Thévenard knocks at the door, enters, and tells the story. Papa immediately bikes to Tata Fanny, to determine our next course of action, if any. That night, indelibly engraved in my memory, we sleep in a barn behind Fanny's house. The bed is narrow. Sandwiched between snoring parents, I keep nocturnal vigil, kicking them periodically, to stop the constant cacophony, only to hear the sound of scurrying mice or rats more clearly . . . *(don't want to know)*. This sleepless night seems endless. When the first rays of the morning sun appear through the cracks of the shutters, and the rooster's call breaks the silence, I jump from bed, quickly throw on some clothes, and ignoring my parents' protests, run to join Florette in her room. Wordlessly, we kneel on the bed and fervently pray for the protection of our god.

Sylvie's whereabouts remained a secret for a long time.

Monsieur Zalman was sent to Auschwitz.

# CHAPTER XII

## THE HIDDEN CHILD

Anne Frank's diary (38) was written by a young teenager, and despite her grave situation, she was able to describe her sentiments and circumstances with touching sensitivity. After reading this book, my own experiences were relived with deep anxiety, as a "hidden child" of the Holocaust. Fortunately for me, the conclusion was far different.

After the Zalman incident, the raids by the milice occurred more frequently. The Chagnons offered to conceal us in their apartment above the shoe store, on the corner of the Place Centrale, very visible to passersby. It was dangerous for them, and their courage under the circumstances is admirable. When I was able to personally express my gratitude to André for his parents' brave actions, many years later, his response was, "C'est le coeur qui parle, il n'y a pas de mérite" (It was done naturally from the heart, it was not done for honors).

My parents gratefully accept the offer, coming clandestinely at night, with few belongings brought by horse and wagon and covered with fresh wood, with the help of André Chagnon and Monsieur Lenoir. Shoes are removed to minimize noise and not worn again until we leave the apartment. Madame Chagnon installs us in her daughter Marcelle's bedroom. I am particularly admonished to speak in whispers and am very frightened. Fingernails are incessantly chewed, to the despair of poor Maman.

During the day, activities are limited to reading or intermittently observing the street's scenes while hidden behind the curtain, only to be scolded and then return to *mon coin* (my corner). Papa reads *Le Petit Dauphinois*, plays solitaire or belote with Mania; Maman knits socks. In the evenings, Monsieur Chagnon brings the radio onto the stairwell leading from the store to the apartment, and we listen secretly to Général de Gaulle and "Les Français parlent aux Français," from London. The Germans attempt to interfere with the broadcast using electrically induced crackling noises but are only partially successful. During an evening transmission, de Gaulle briefly provides a hopeful, spiritually uplifting prediction of French life after the war. Monsieur Chagnon and Papa discuss the news. It seems de Gaulle and Général Giraud are vying for the presidency of the CLN (Comité de Libération Nationale), and the adults are pleased at de Gaulle's success. Hearing Radio London is exciting, especially since it is forbidden.

The days pass so slowly! Even the thought of school is pleasant. I miss Florette. Periodically, Marcelle Chagnon, André's sister, joins us upstairs after the day's work, with a pictorial distraction, however inappropriate. The three-dimensional photographs of horribly mutilated French soldiers in the trenches in World War I fascinate but only add to my worries. Marcelle means well.

On my visit to Yenne in 2000, I asked André about these images. They had been retained, but I had no desire to view them again. We reminisced about Marcelle who died at the age of twenty after a brief marriage and a severely complicated pregnancy. Madame Chagnon never recovered, conversing with her daughter during our later visits, as if she were present in the room. André appeared grim and sad on hearing the name of his sister. The subject was quickly dropped.

In 1943, André is a cute young man in his early twenties, with a charming and mischievous smile, who, when not dodging the SOT (*Service Obligatoire du Travail*), works in his father's store. Once during our concealment, he knocks softly on the door and cautions that an electrician is coming to repair a wire adjacent to our room. The upper portion of the door consists of a glass window pane which could betray us to someone on a stepladder. The four of us crouch near the door while the electrician is working. André converses and jokes to distract his attention.

"J'peux vous offrir un petit canon?" (Will you have a drink?), says André.

"Ah! j'dis pas non!" (I won't refuse).

Sweat drips from Father's forehead. I can hardly breathe, let alone speak, wrapped in Maman's tight grip, her lips softly kissing my hair, whispering to be quiet. The electrician completes the work, and all heave a sigh of relief. We return to our house two weeks later.

This last experience so increases my fear that I now sleep with my mother while Father uses my bed. Nightmares are frequent. One recurs: Gestapo agents wrench the door open.

"Please don't take my parents," I cry.

"Which one do you want to remain?" they ask.

Unable to make a choice, I chase the truck carrying them away and then awaken screaming, "They are knocking at the door! They are here to take us!"

My parents are at a loss. Papa suggests a return to the *paysan* family in the mountains, but Maman disagrees. It is finally decided to leave me with the Thomases, the grocers who also have a store on the Place Centrale, near the fountain. I don't want to go but am literally dragged, weeping to Madame Thomas whose soft embrace is soothing and consoling. Soon daughters Janine and Michèle join us. Tante Marie, Madame Thomas' sister, attempts (without success) to be amusing. After some urging, Maman leaves reluctantly. Although in perpetual disagreement, this is our first separation. Madame Thomas and the girls make silly faces and offer to play games, finally inducing my laughter . . . . Michèle's first communion takes place the next day, a prospect for a happy celebration. The sisters are a few years older. The three of us bathe in the kitchen, in a large copper tub filled with kettles of heated water, preparing for the big event. Later I am lying in bed between my two new friends. Michèle and Janine turn each on their side and murmur, "Sainte Marie, Mère de Dieu, priez pour nous, pauvres pécheurs, aujourd'hui et à l'heure de notre mort. Que Jésus, le Fruit de vos Entrailles, soit béni." The prayer finished, a quick, "Bonne nuit," and silence. Soon, they are both asleep. I am awake throughout the night, thinking of their prayer, so foreign to my ears, listening to their quiet breathing, and expectantly to the church bells tolling every fifteen minutes. I find myself counting the twelve midnight bells. At last, dozing off at daybreak, I am aroused by Michèle's cheerful "Get ready for church!" Maman had fashioned a pleated little pink dress for special events. Madame Thomas combs and brushes my hair but does not attach the big bow.

This is my first experience in a Catholic church. The little girls wear white tulle dresses with veils and look like ballerinas. The boys are also very attractive in their black suits, with a white satin ribbon and bow on one arm! Advancing down the aisle, with the choir singing, they look very solemn and proud of their newfound importance. Their baptism is being renewed by professing their faith. Then, the meaning of the first communion is unknown to me. I listen attentively to the priest performing the mass in Latin. The people kneel, stand up, chant, kneel, and rise again. It is a beautiful pageant. I am envious. Why can't I be Catholic? Then, remembering the Jewish god worshipped with Florette, I decide to remain standing, with head held high, put my hands together while the congregation is kneeling and bent forward in supplication. Some stare, wondering at my lack of participation, but defiant, I don't care. Tears well in my eyes. I too am praying, begging God to keep my family and friends safe.

The family returns to the Thomas apartment behind the grocery, where a large feast has been prepared. The guests gorge themselves with mounds of hors d'oeuvre, fowl, beef, rabbit, venison, vegetables, potatoes, and cake, washed down with a variety of white, red, and rosé wines and champagne. The noise level rises, along with flushing cheeks, mine included. Risqué jokes and songs flow unabated. The gaiety is contagious, and I join in; the priest too.

In church again, at 4:00 PM for Vespers. Everyone is tipsy . . . the priest too. I loudly sing along with the congregants, which amuses the Thomases, forgetting, at least for the moment, prior fears and discomfort. Staggering back to the house, Michèle, Janine, and I totter to our room, laugh while undressing, and finally slip into bed. I immediately fall asleep, vaguely aware of the girls' softly spoken prayers, only to be sharply awakened by the disturbing church bells, as if a reminder that the wonderful day has been just a respite. Troubling thoughts quickly return, and the nightmare relived: *Will the Germans come while I am away? Who will be taken? Who will I choose? I am convinced that Papa and Maman are already gone. I don't care about Mania who is always arguing, criticizing, and only listens to Papa. I've got to return home.*

The church bells continue to toll, and dawn comes slowly. Although the celebrants have not fully recovered from the previous day's celebration, it is now Monday; the Thomas' store is open for business, and the sisters go to school. Arriving early at the house to Maman's surprise, I cry.

"Maman, I want to remain here with you. If the Gestapo takes us, they'll take us all, but I don't want to be without you."

"Oy, Gevalt! Mine kindele!" cries Maman, hugging me tightly.

Nevertheless, the war of the cuticles continues, unabated. Maman does not understand that my anxieties concerning our dangerous situation, confusion about religion and anti-Semitism at school, and conflicts with Mania are expressed by nail-biting.

Would she love me more if I were a cripple? The idea flourishes in my imagination.

I dramatically collapse one day, on the playground, relishing the attention. Scarcely able to walk, I am accompanied by my playmates and Madame Moliaix. Frantic, Maman makes inquiries and finds a physician in Aix-Les-Bains, to which we travel by bus. It smells of diesel oil, the cheapest fuel available. The bus is stopped at the tunnel of the Dent du Chat by the police patrol, to verify the papers of the passengers. Hands shaking, Maman nervously provides the identity card conspicuously stamped

Yenne at Michèle Thomas' first communion me, left of
the picture, Michèle, Janine, and friends

Yenne: Place Centrale.
The Thomas grocery was to the left of the flower display

"JUIF" and the pass from Langlois with a shaky smile. It is not returned. The police give us just a cursory look. This is very surprising as the worst is expected in these circumstances. Since then, men in uniform cause me to feel guilty, for no apparent reason, perhaps because of such past experiences. I sometimes ponder on the thoughts of the French police when coming upon Jewish travelers and hopefully believe that some of these men, especially those not in the milice, must have felt sympathy as well as shame, witnessing our humiliation and fear.

On arrival at the doctor's office, the symptoms are gone. The doctor diagnoses my ailment as "growing pains." In any case, I enjoy the day away from school. Maman's attention and love are mine exclusively. So relieved by the diagnosis, she celebrates by stopping at a *Pâtisserie* and a bookstore on the main avenue. Aix-les-Bains is a spectacle in itself. There are few cars on the street, mostly bikes and bicycle-taxis. The latter are driven by poor men pedaling for a living. I feel sorry for them. There are young men and women strolling in the streets, wearing strange clothing. At least, they seem odd to me, having lived in a small town and among farmers. Maman laughs at my bewildered look and exclaims, "C'est les Zazous!" (It's the Zootsuiters!) What's that? "They rebel against society and dress accordingly—long jackets with drooping or exaggerated square shoulders, short trousers, large shoes, and striped socks. They definitely make a statement to the 'enemy,' swinging never-opened umbrellas, as if to say, '*tuh mir eppess!*' (do me something)." Each generation has its own version of the Zazous.

Returning home later that day, I relate these adventures to Papa and Mania, who are relieved to see us safe.

The leg pains are gone.

However, the enemy was not.

During one of my post-war visits in Yenne, I asked my friend André Chagnon, still handsome, a spry, white-haired, tanned seventy-year-old, "Did you know who the collaborators were?"

"Many of them disappeared," André answered with an ironic smile. "At the end of the war, some were hidden at the Abbaye de Hautecombe situated on the lake of Aix-les-Bains, le Lac du Bourget. You know about Touvier (40), don't you? He was hidden by the monks after the war. I remember them. They came to my father to have their boots repaired, in exchange for cigarettes. The bad guys were known to us, but they were not discussed. Even now."

"Why?"

"Ça remue de mauvais souvenirs, et personne ne veut en parler" (It stirs up bad memories, and nobody wants to talk about them).

As André spoke about Touvier, the name of Maurice Papon came to mind, another Vichyite who took part in the deportation of Jews.(39)

Tante Marie, then a sweet ninety-year-old lady, was also present during our conversation and added, "Madame Pouchois a caché les Oppenheimer dans une chambre au deuxième. Parfois il lui fallait des légumes. Elle me disait, 'Marie, donne-moi quelque chose.' Je savais, bien qu'elle ne m'ait rien dit." (Madame Pouchois hid the Oppenheimers in a second-floor room. Sometimes, she needed vegetables and would say, 'Marie, give me something.' I understood, although she told me nothing.)

Tante Marie spoke of the Oppenheimers, who had been good friends of the Zalmans. The daughter had been deported. Anita had been a great beauty, and Tante Marie surmised that she had been chosen for reproduction or worse, in the concentration camp. She continued, with tears in her eyes, "One early morning, they came for the son, Werner. He jumped out the window, trying to escape, was caught by the milice dressed only in shirt and pants, and cried, 'Maman, Maman!'" Tante Marie was sobbing. "I saw everything and could do nothing. The poor mother, disheveled, in her night clothes, was sitting on a rock in front of the house, crushed with grief, wailing and begging for her son's freedom. They are all dead now. The parents are buried in Yenne." Later, I discovered that another daughter, Dorothée, had survived.

Then, we kept quiet. *Les murs ont des oreilles* (the walls have ears) was the constant motto. It seems strange to reflect on this so many years later. Names, which became infamous, such as Touvier, Papon, and Klaus Barbie were unknown to us at the time. On our last visit to the Savoie, in June 2000, Michèle and Janine Thomas organized an excursion to Izieu, a village about twenty-five miles from Yenne. Izieu is now a French national shrine memorializing the fate of Jewish children and adults who were captured there and deported by the Nazis.

The Sous-Préfet of Belley, Pierre Marcel Wilzer had provided a house in this isolated mountain village to Sabine Zlatin (a Red Cross nurse) and her husband Miron (an agricultural engineer) who founded *La colonie des enfants refugiés de l'HERAULT*, in April 1943, a refuge and school for Jewish children whose parents were either deported or who wanted to assure their safety. The *chef du cabinet* of the Préfet of Chambéry, Alain Mousse (40), was in charge of the *Oeuvre de Secours des Enfants* (aid for children) and distributed false passports to the children of Izieu to go to Switzerland. During breakfast, on Holy Thursday of April 6, 1944, Klaus Barbie (41) came with the milice and Gestapo to arrest forty-four children and seven adults. The director and two boys were taken to the fortress of Revel and shot. On April 15, 1944, forty-one children and five adults died in the gas chamber in Auschwitz, nine days after their arrest. One of the teachers who had escaped, and Madame Zlatin, the sole survivor of those arrested, testified during Barbie's trial. A monument was erected upon the direction of François Mitterand, president of France, at a distance from the house, facing the beautiful, peaceful valley. It reads: "La République Française, en hommages aux victimes des persécutions racistes et antisémites, et crimes contre l'Humanité, commis avec la complicité du Gouvernement de Vichy, dit 'Gouvernement de l'Etat Français,'" *(1940–1944)*. *N'oublions jamais* (The French Republic, in homage to the victims of racist and anti-Semitic persecutions and crimes against humanity, committed with the complicity of the government of Vichy, said: "Government of the French State" [1940–1944]. We shall never forget). Izieu was so close to Yenne, and yet we never knew.

André Chagnon presented me with a memoir (42) written by Rachel Perelstein. She lived in Moutiers during World War II. Her parents had been taken to the concentration camps, and she and her sister were hidden by a Christian maquisard (member of the Résistance), whom she married at the end of the war, after having fought in the *Maquis* herself. Her story tells of the occupation in Moutiers, which served as a Nazi headquarters. Yenne was also very close to Moutiers. Fate here again kept us unaware and relatively safe.

*Why was my family spared?*

Before leaving Yenne, I made a pilgrimage to the town's cemetery with my husband, experiencing such sadness, that his support was essential. After searching for a while, the gravesite of the Oppenheimers was finally found, among all the crosses. Its sole headstone was engraved with a Star of David, their names, and those of their deported daughter and son.

Ironically, Werner's epitaph read: "Mort pour la France" (Died for France).

**Yenne: The Oppenheimer gravesite**

School at Izieu

A LA MÉMOIRE
DU DIRECTEUR, DU PERSONNEL
ET DES ÉLÈVES
DE CETTE ÉCOLE
ARRÊTÉS EN 1943 ET 1944
PAR LA POLICE DE VICHY
ET LA GESTAPO
DÉPORTÉS ET EXTERMINÉS
À AUSCHWITZ
PARCE QUE NÉS JUIFS

Memorial plaque on wall of school of Izieu

# CHAPTER XIII

## THE END OF THE NIGHTMARE

Despite the Demarcation Line supposedly dividing France into the Occupied and Free Zones, the Vichy government was de facto, largely under Nazi control since the Armistice. In 1943, Germany had already suffered disaster in Russia, at Stalingrad. The path to eventual defeat had begun.

During this period, the *Maquis* (French Résistance) was becoming an increasingly prominent factor. At first, many anti-Nazi Frenchmen were uncertain whether Vichy was the enemy but soon learned differently with the imposition of dictatorial policies restricting individual freedoms. Young patriots, communists, and former extreme right-wing conservatives joined the Résistance early on. Vichy did not regard them as a Résistance movement but rather, as *brigands*. When the SOT began to pursue a policy of forced labor for the Nazis, thousands of Frenchmen inhabiting the mountainous regions disappeared to join the *Maquis* in the Alps, and other mountainous regions of France. (43) It was best not to know their whereabouts. Anyone arrested by the Gestapo could be tortured to obtain information.

During a visit to Yenne in June 2000, Tante Marie reminisced with André Chagnon of the occasions when the maquisards, who were quartered in Vertemex, a neighboring mountain village, came to the Thomas' grocery at night, to stock up on food and candles and slept there. It soon became apparent that there were significant political differences between the Résistance groups of the Left and Right, resulting in the formation of anti-communist countermaquis and subsequent armed conflict between them. Discussion concerning the Résistance at the time by family and friends was not understandable to me. (43)

The principal daily preoccupation for us was survival, in 1943 and 1944.

Fascist Italy capitulates in September 1943. Aix-Les-Bains becomes a recuperation center for approximately two thousand German occupation forces whose physicians inhabit the Hôtel du Parc. Headquarters is at the Hôtel Albion. The *Kommandantur* (German headquarters) also takes over the Hôtel des Thermes. This is complemented by the Gestapo and French Milice in Chambéry. Dussuel, mayor of Aix-les-Bains, is pro-Vichy. Concomitantly the FFI (maquisards) distribute information, indoctrinate, and train new recruits fleeing forced labor (SOT), help receive Allied agents and supplies parachuted to the Savoie and other areas of France (44), and carry out acts of sabotage. The Germans finally occupy the so-called Free Zone, still referred to as "Free" for Vichy's sake. It is certainly not free for the Jews because the raids on their known locations accelerate.

The local *Mairie* projects German propaganda films and newsreels at the city hall where the audience noisily moves benches to face the screen and impatiently awaits the feature film. The family takes part chiefly due to curiosity and boredom, and because Papa enjoys movies and misses this form of entertainment. The Germans always appear victorious in the news film. The narrator does not mention German defeats on the Eastern Front: "A l'Est, rien de nouveau" (Nothing new on the Eastern Front), he says.

*La Fille au Vautour* is particularly well remembered, concerning a wholesome German girl with plaited blond hair who flees to the mountains with a tame eagle to escape an unwanted marriage. Eventually, the story ends well, as the heroine returns home to marry the man she loves and releases the eagle. While speculative, the tame eagle could represent latent Nazi power (after overwhelming domination of Europe). The blond girl appears to symbolize pure Aryan virtue. This film is nowadays considered a "masterwork of the period," a genre very popular in Germany as a *Heimat film* (concerning "the Homeland"). Then, these images had no meaning for me. Retrospectively, I find it amazing that unattractive individuals such as Hitler, Goering, Bormann, Himmler, and others in this clique, given their physical appearance and stature, could be perceived as belonging to the so-called Aryan master race.

Much of my free time was spent with Aunt Fanny and her family. Maman, whose depression was apparent, slept in the afternoons. Papa read or played cards with Mania or Mr. Mirrelwasser, having been unsuccessful at gardening. Unhappy and anxious, it is not surprising that my parents developed high blood pressure and rheumatism because of constant stress, humidity, lack of exercise, and improper diet. Fearing arrest by the Gestapo or milice, they could not readily consult physicians in Aix-Les-Bains and instead used the local doctor, Dr. Prunier, a tall skinny man, who made house visits. On such an occasion, I recall him examining my mother by, reluctantly and timidly lifting her pendulous breast in order to auscultate her heart and lungs. Papa, Mania, and I would exchange smiles, and Maman would bite her lip to avoid laughing. These examinations usually resulted in the therapeutic application of leeches to the arms and legs. The repulsive, black-skinned, crawling, bloodsucking mini-Draculas supposedly lowered blood pressure. *Ventouses* were *de rigueur* for bronchitis and pneumonia. These cupping glasses were heated inverted on a Bunsen burner, whereupon Dr. Prunier (unconcernedly) would quickly attach them to Maman's back, which produced a red skin welt, purportedly to reduce congestion and inflammation. This procedure was also horrifying, and I refused similar treatment. Maman insisted on smelly mustard plasters applied to the chest instead. The choice of doctors was extremely limited. The other local physician had even a worse reputation; one of his patients allegedly died of a ruptured appendix.

With these dubious alternatives, it was advisable to obtain a reliable physician in Aix-les-Bains. However, because a permit was needed, and due to the increased dangers associated with travel, my parents decided not to proceed. Many of the Jews who attempted a visit to Lyon, Grenoble, Aix, or Chambéry often did not return. Such was the case in Yenne involving a man who had gone to Chambéry. His poor wife was left alone without financial means. The Jewish community in the village rallied together to help. My Christian friends have often remarked about the solidarity of the Jews during these hard times.

A partial reopening of the French-Swiss border in February 1944 encouraged Papa to seek entry permits. The Swiss were reticent to issue permits to Jewish refugees, having to contend with the restrictive policies of the adjacent Nazi regime and problems in providing food and shelter. Families were allowed to cross the border if they included children under six years of age. Papa still could not bear the thought of departing his *chère* (dear) France. Traditionally optimistic, he believed that the Allies were winning the war and considered immigration unnecessary. Maman did not agree. The family did not qualify anyway since I was now twelve. Papa had learned of the many Jewish orphans, especially in Nice, resulting from the frequent parental deportations. Papa and Maman were ready to adopt such a child in order to cross the border. Little cousins Marc and Michel did qualify. The three families began the process of obtaining false documents for everyone, since the identity cards stamped "JUIF" were not useable. Acting on information within the Jewish community, Papa traveled to Chambéry and returned with the falsified documents.

Maman and Mania's knowledge of the French language was extremely basic, their accents even worse. They struggled to recall and pronounce their new names. Papa half-jokingly admonished them. Mania obeyed quickly. Maman flirted with a mischievous smile, batting her eyes, purposely mispronouncing her bogus name, date of birth, address, exaggerating already heavily accented French. Although the situation was serious, evenings were spent at Tata Fanny's, practicing, and there was general amusement at Maman's antics. This effort was for naught because the news from the Thévenards and the BBC indicated that the end of the war may be approaching.

Rouen, Paris, and in Toulon suburbs are bombarded, as well as French industries, especially the Renault factories near Paris. Possible invasion by the Allies is discussed. There is a massacre of French civilians by the Germans in Oradour-sur-Glane (45), and a general mobilization of the milice to oppose the *Maquis*. Information about concentration camps and the slaughter of Jews begin leaking out.

Finally, *le Jour J*, or D-Day! June 6, 1944, Operation Overlord. The Allies invade Normandy. The BBC news reports that Bayeux, Cherbourg, and Caen in ruins are liberated. During the battles, the Germans send their healthy troops to fight and attempt to evacuate their wounded. The victory in Avranches opens the road to Paris. Names such as Eisenhower, Leclerc (46), de Lattre de Tassigny, and Churchill dominate our thoughts and conversation. On the same day (June 6, 1944), the maquisards sabotage tunnels, bridges, railroad tracks, and telephone lines. The German response is violent. At the nearby village of Chaumette, in reprisal, the Gestapo chief, Heinsen, shoots eighteen hostages after forcibly having them dig their own graves. The sole escapee is ironically a Jew, Wirtheimer, who relates the story.(47)

In August 1944, there is an insurrection by the Résistance in Paris. The Germans surrender to Général Leclerc. Paris is liberated. For those in Yenne, it reaffirms that the end of the war may be in sight. *La Libération de Paris* is unforgettable. I bike through the streets, screaming, "Paris est libre." The Yennois fill doorways, laughing and kissing one another. The Germans are retreating, and radios are blaring. The events are now fast paced. London is attacked by V1 and V2 rockets. Lyon is liberated; so is Toulon. Germany continues to be bombarded by the Allies. De Gaulle, now in Paris, has traveled through France in triumph and forms a coalition government with the Leftist political parties.(48), Collaborators are beaten. Women who slept with the enemy are paraded in the streets, naked, with hair shaven. (49)

At the Col du Chat, André Chagnon and two other maquisards hold approximately twenty German prisoners. One of his companions is rough with the prisoners because his family had been killed by the Nazis. It is also a potentially dangerous situation since the Frenchmen are considerably outnumbered. However, they do not try to escape, probably weary of the war and their own defeat. One of the Germans plays the accordion. André remembers sharing food and cigarettes with them. In spite of the hostility created by past events, André admits that it was difficult for him to be cruel. Although he hated the Germans in general, the prisoners were considered as individuals, and sometimes it was forgotten that they were the enemy. As a child, I dreamt of butchering Hitler, but as an adult, I can empathize with André's sentiments. Immediately after the war, I was unable and unwilling to face or address a German. All I could see were swastikas. The passage of time tempered my anger and hatred against the entire German people.

On reflection: How would I have acted during the Occupation? Would I have put myself or my family at risk to protect someone or to fight in the Resistance? I hope so but don't know for certain. During the Occupation, fear ruled. André Chagnon, his family, the Moliaixes, the Thevenards and the Thomases have not only my gratitude, but also my admiration for their humanity and courage.

In Yenne, the police chief, in the last months of 1944, changes his political allegiance. Travel permits are not so difficult to obtain. The gloomy atmosphere at home gradually dissipates. Maman is subject to frenzied cursing for little apparent reason. Hitler, as well as Langlois, are the recipients. In June, de Gaulle leads a victory parade in Paris, which is also celebrated in Yenne. "La Marseillaise," this revolutionary song expressing in its fierce lyrics a hatred of the monarchy of the eighteenth century, and now so relevant, is sung in the school yard and streets by townspeople, arms entwined, shouting with joy: "Aux Armes, Citoyens" (To

Arms, Citizens!). Yes! Indeed! My voice is hoarse, but nevertheless I continue to scream: "Liberté, liberté chérie," another verse of the anthem. How good it feels. Even now, a sense of victory and revenge is experienced on hearing the words of the "Marseillaise." Many years later, when teaching the French national anthem to American students, these emotions were imparted to them, and their joyous strident voices resonated in the school's corridors.

On the Place Centrale, effigies of Hitler are burned, accompanied by the sounds of, "*A bas Hitler*" (down with Hitler). A month later, on July 14, the first Bastille Day is celebrated since the war began, with dancing in the streets and on the Place Centrale, to the sounds of the local brass band. Hiroshima and Nagasaki have been bombed by the Americans and "La Danse Atomique" is cynically in fashion. Adrienne Lenoir prances happily about in a flowery cotton dress and has many dance partners. Florette, Aimée, and I sigh and dance with each other.

Tata Fanny has encouraged us to keep a journal. It records: *Tomorrow is a big day. Rumor has it that the Americans and the FFI (Forces Françaises de l'Intérieur) are to come through the village tomorrow. I shall finally be able to show off my English. Florette and I dress in blue, white, and red, the colors of the French flag, and stand along with other Yennois on the Avenue des Platanes, on the outskirts of the village, near the Rhône river. Ready for the parade, we wait and wait, looking forward to chewing gum and chocolate that the Americans supposedly distribute from their military vehicles. I have never eaten chocolate, first because Maman does not want me to ruin my teeth, but mostly because there is none. I rehearse what I am going to say in English to the Americans: "Thank you for saving us." We stand there in vain. They did not pass through Yenne! But I shall continue to study English; I want to.*

The first deportees are coming back from Ravensbrück, Auschwitz, Buchenwald, and other concentration camps.

French prisoners of war are returning also. Conversation in the shops on the Place Centrale predominantly concentrates on the poor, lost, forlorn, shuffling, skeletonlike, sick people dressed in rags or striped uniforms. There is a shared, morbid curiosity. Maman is interested in determining what happened in the camps, although Papa, equally interested, does not say anything. As fate would have it, we are suddenly contacted by Madame Zalman who informs us that her husband David survived Auschwitz. They rented an apartment in Aix-Les-Bains. Maman and I are invited to Sylvie's eleventh birthday celebration. It is relaxing to be unconcerned with permits, the milice, and Gestapo. Sylvie and I are delighted to see each other again. She has invited a boy, the son of her mother's friend. He is cute, I think. Sylvie agrees. He is the topic of our conversation. We giggle, gazing shyly his way from time to time. I am thirteen, a gawky teenager.

"Sylvie, where is your papa?" I finally ask.

"Papa does not want to come out of his room."

"Why?"

"I don't know. He won't talk to anybody."

Madame Zalman relates that after David was taken, her mother and Sylvie were sent to a convent. Monsieur Zalman was interned at Ruffieux, a regroupment camp for deportees before shipment to Drancy and then to the concentration camps in Germany and Poland. Madame Zalman's efforts to have him released by the Préfecture de Police in Chambéry were futile. Madame Zalman rejoined her daughter and mother. Maman does not question further.

The party goes on. Cakes and tea are served. Maman demands that I recite a fable by Jean de la Fontaine.

" . . . Fernande is wonderful," brags my mother, "and so cute . . . ." I glance at Sylvie and her *petit ami* (boyfriend), roll my eyes, and comply. "Le Corbeau et le Renard" is narrated with emotion. I enjoy the attention, and the fable is funny. As the fox flatters and tricks the crow in order to steal his cheese, Monsieur Zalman silently appears at the bedroom door, listens to the recital, applauds, and exclaims with a smile, "A scheyne meydele!" (Pretty girl!) Sylvie and I hurry to him and are hugged in return. He is also embraced by Maman. All present are deeply moved. The man is haggard, emaciated, and hardly recognizable, with a facial expression of profound grief. This man, who could always joke, is deeply depressed and exhausted. A red scar above the upper lip is a reminder of the torture he endured . . . the SS beat him before deserting the camp, he states reluctantly. Madame Zalman urges him to go back to bed. The despair in his eyes is haunting. Never again did he utter a word about Auschwitz in our presence.

\*   \*   \*

On returning from school, on April 12, 1945, Maman is crying. "Roosevelt, the savior of the Jews, is dead." The death of the American president has a somber effect on the Jewish families and the townspeople in general. Only later did I feel great disappointment, learning that President Roosevelt only belatedly attempted to relieve the plight of European Jewry.

The war is over. Yenne is festive: there will be a fair on the *Champ de Foire* for a week, with merry-go-rounds, shooting galleries, and *auto tamponnantes* (electric cars). Never have there been so many people on the Champ de Foire, at one time. The noise is deafening, expressing the town's exultation. "What fun it is to drive these electric cars that bump into one another." Florette and I good-naturedly argue as to the driver; we alternate. Laughing, screaming, and crashing into the side of the arena, we so enjoyed the ride that Papa has difficulty removing us from the small vehicle. This festive event heralds the end of our stay in Yenne.

Papa has returned to Paris with Mania to help find an apartment. There is a large family celebration before their departure. Unfortunately, the chickens and geese can't accompany us. Maman has *La Belle*, and *La Patronne* sacrificed by our neighbor, and tearfully prepares them for dinner. No one is able to eat. The cooked chickens are given to the Lenoirs, who also adopt the geese with our blessing. I feel relieved! At least they will have a family.

After great anticipation, a letter from Papa finally arrives: *I am at last settling the score with Claude and Max,* he writes. *In the meantime, there is an international conference on reparations. The indemnity of occupation reaches five hundred million francs. The factory is back in our hands, and Magnin did not put up too much of a fuss. Max and I return to work. It is wonderful. Mania has found an apartment in Levallois, near la Porte Champerret, the northwest end of Paris. I think you will like it. It's time to pack everything and come here. I am looking for a lycée for Fifi. The schools are full, and it is very difficult nowadays in Paris. Food is available only on the black market, but you know Mania. When it comes to food, she'll find it. I saw Fanny, Suzanne, and their families. Fanny has to settle her affairs but found her old flat intact. She wants a divorce from Georges, who has suddenly reappeared. She desires no further contact with him; neither do the children. She is seeking a job, and I am helping in this regard. Suzanne also restarts her life by taking over the fur business that Emile began before the hostilities. Jean and Jeannette are back from Pau with the children. Jean has found his old apartment undamaged and can also begin again. He is a good tailor and is making a new suit for me which I need for the factory!*

*No news from my sister Régine and her family! They'll never come back. I have heard from my sister Rosa. She is still in Belgium with Isaac, but they hope to join their sons, Sigi and Sami, who are in Palestine in the British Army. Marthe, Nadine, and their families returned from Cannes where they spent the war years, as well as Madame Robert and her children, Marcel and Monique. Eveline and Isidore died in concentration camps. And here is more sad news: Monsieur Robert and Marcel, his son, fought in the Maquis, using the names of de Signac. Apparently, having a non-Jewish name in the Maquis was preferable. Was it anti-Semitism or self-protection if apprehended? Unfortunately, Monsieur Robert tragically was killed in action.*

*I keep searching for news of our relatives. Nothing from Poland or Lithuania. We'll continue seeking.*

*How is my Fifi? Come back quickly.*

Maman and I cry after reading the letter. I remember François and our war games. What has happened to all of them? We shall never know.

Having lived in dread for four years, we're happy to say goodbye to Yenne. I can't wait to return to Paris and a new life. After packing our belongings and bidding our friends and neighbors farewell, we depart. There are not many trains in service. During the war, the railroad was frequently sabotaged. The cars are packed with people and luggage. Suitcases placed in the aisles are used as seats. The bathroom door is unhinged. French soldiers act as shields, providing privacy when Maman and I require use of the facility. The passengers are so elated by the events that despite the many inconveniences, there is no impatience or hostility, only goodwill. The mood is jovial; few sleep. The nightmare is finally over!

Ecstatic, we arrive in Paris. Due to the dense crowds, the luggage, Maman, and I exit through the windows, passing one by one into Papa's arms.

*Vive la Liberté*!

# CHAPTER XIV

## TRAPPED

Had I been a Catholic and/or an aristocrat whose lineage was traceable to medieval time, life would have been easier. Hitler probably would have left my family in peace. The Second World War would be recalled as a terrible period in world history, but far less personal.

As a teenager, I hated my name and Father's "naturalized" French citizenship, but above all, being Jewish. Imagined was a bistro sign proclaiming: "Chez Fernande," with the namesake serving apéritifs at the *zinc* (slang for a bar covered by zinc) to the local customers. There is nothing wrong about serving apéritifs, mind you, but I longed to have an aristocratic title, as proudly held by many characters in French literature. Actually, I was named after my deceased grandfather, Ephraim, following Jewish tradition, which requires, at least in theory, the same first initial. Therefore, why not an $E$ as in Elise, which is so distinguished, rather than paradoxically an $F$ for Fernande? Even stranger, my Yiddish name, Frume (Hassidah in Hebrew), does not bear the proper initial either. It ironically means "The Pious One"; I am anything but devout.

To make matters worse, the family name, Horensztajn, retains all the Polish consonants. Can you imagine a Frenchman pronouncing them? Impossible! Even the most learned professor would falter over the last syllable and mumble, "Horen . . . quoi?"

(what?) Embarrassingly, I had to contend with snickering fellow students and timidly but courteously attempted to correct the professor who was "botching" my name. Gosh! Only to be an Odile de Broglie, a classmate whose parents undoubtedly had their name printed in the *Bottin Mondain* (The Social Register), belonged to the Racing Club de France, resided in Auteuil or near the Bois de Boulogne. The "Horenstajn's" apartment, in contrast, was located in Levallois, a working-class suburb bordering these select and elite districts. The French *particule*, *de*, denotes noble background. The family's name is also difficult to pronounce: "de Broeye" and not "de Broglee." Her father and grandfather were famous scientists! Mine were of humble origin and uneducated, who escaped the pogroms in Poland and Lithuania. What's in a name? I must admit that my future husband's family name was definitely an attraction. Wagman was simpler than Horenstajn, any day.

Peer acceptance was my goal, quite difficult with a name like Horen . . . *quoi*? I always felt inferior and an outsider in my own country, longing to be a true Frenchman, envying Pierre Mendès-France, a prime minister's in the 1950s, most well known in the USA for unsuccessfully attempting to replace wine with milk in schools. Here was a Jewish hero of the Resistance whose family roots could be traced back to fifteenth-century France.

It was difficult to be Jewish, growing up in France during and after World War II. Religion, for many Jews, was largely ignored or denied. I enrolled in a private school in which most students were children of affluent bourgeois of the Seventeenth Arrondissement. Here was Fernande Horen . . . *quoi*, a frumpily dressed cute, petite French Jewish girl, with bushy hair à la Einstein, lacking verbal and social skills. She is invited by a *de* person to a *surprise partie* on Avenue Foch, near the Arc de Triomphe. Papa wants to meet the parents of her host. "No way," she says. "I'll pick you up at eleven in the evening," Papa says. "Too early, midnight," she protests. Papa surrenders.

He should have never left.

The *partie* goes downhill from the moment of arrival in this stuffy, antique-filled apartment. The parents are absent, *le whiskee* is flowing, and many guests are already tipsy, making out here and there.

"Ah! Voilà la youpine!" (Here is the kike!)

"Ta gueule! Elle entend!" (Shut up! She hears!)

"Et alors?" (So what?)

I hear the boys' comments, and humiliated, I try to hide my despair by showing apparent interest in the floral design decorating the beautiful harpsichord standing near an armchair. *I wish to leave.* The host, slightly drunk, invites me to dance. Boogie-woogie is a current favorite. I am temporarily exhilarated by the lively rhythm of "Bugle Boy of Company B." Afterward, I wait impatiently, and a sigh of relief greets Papa's return. My acceptance by the "group" at subsequent *surprise parties* did not improve. Although anti-Semitic jokes were hurtful, in cowardly fashion, I would laugh along and hate myself later for doing so.

Catholicism was attractive. Some catechism, as well as portions of the New Testament, were well known to me, long before setting eyes on "The Five Books of Moses." Papa used to say, "Thank God, I am an atheist." Maman had created a brief, unique religious/cultural philosophy of her own. She did not smoke on Saturdays, fasted on Yom Kippur, and cooked *gefilte fish* for all the major Jewish holidays.

I remember discovering a copy of the New Testament in the attic in Yenne and found the name Jesus. Having been told by schoolmates on many occasions that I personally had killed *le Petit Jésus*, the book was brought to Papa who was asked, "Who is Jesus?" Maman, always prone to temper tantrums when faced with such delicate situations, began to yell hysterically, as if my conversion was imminent.

"Jesus," Papa answered after a few seconds of hesitation, not paying attention to her, "was a very good man. The Christians believe in him, and we Jews do not." This simple explanation surprisingly satisfied my curiosity.

"Papa, people say that I killed him."

"No, you did not. The anti-Semites say that. Don't listen to them."

"What are anti-Semites?"

"People who don't like Jews."

Once again, a very simple, concise answer. Papa always looked so sure of himself that his words had to be the truth. A few weeks later, Papa bought me a children's Bible. The wonderful stories in the Old Testament were exciting and pleasurable. I especially liked the romantic tale of Ruth and Boaz. This young woman who loved Boaz was willing to leave her people and cultural heritage for him. Reaching maturity without learning about the historical and religious traditions of Judaism could later have easily caused me to emulate the story of Ruth, by marrying a non-Jew. However, Papa was my idol; I could never knowingly hurt him. Perhaps this is why, although tempted, I neither converted nor married out of the faith and, in fact, initially had decided never to marry at all. Besides, it was too difficult to remain faithful to just one person for a lifetime. And Maman was forever harping about having *a goy* for a son-in-law!

"What will you do if I bring you a Christian son-in-law, Papa?"

"You know that your mother will be very unhappy."

"And you?"

"Well, to tell you the truth, it would be preferable if you married a Jew, but I shall never deny you, as our daughter."

How disappointing for an avid young reader to become aware that some favorite writers were Catholic and anti-Semitic. An unpleasant Jewish character or a prejudicial remark in a story would cause me to feel dejected, and angry at the author as well as myself, resembling in a sense, Estelle in *Huis Clos (No Exit)*, Jean-Paul Sartre's play, who could only visualize herself as reflected by the opinions of Garcin and Ines. These characters imprisoned in a room with no exit are dependent on one another and despise this dependence, discovering that they are in Hell, and that, "Hell is the Others" (*L'Enfer, c'est les autres*). Only once

Paris, after the war
"Cours Félix"—Private school. With schoolmates.

Winter in Megeve
1946
with Florette

does the door to their room open, providing the opportunity to leave. They choose to remain because of fear of the unknown outside.

Similarly, I was in a hell, imprisoned by Jewishness, with no way out.

The Cours Félix was at the fringe of elite society. The student body was taught elegant manners: a quick *reverence* for girls, a bow at the waist for boys to which was added, as they grew older, *le baise-main* (kissing of the lady's hand). The school was situated above a *boulangerie* (bakery) from which wafted delicious aromas. Unable to resist, the students bought warm, melt-in-the-mouth, buttery croissants devoured at recess. Nearby was a *charcuterie* (delicatessen) and *crèmerie* (cheese shop) where Maman shopped weekly. She insisted on accompanying to and fetching me from school, over which there were numerous arguments. It was for my protection, she declared. White slavery was her concern. This overprotectiveness was emotionally paralyzing. The resulting insecurities were sublimated by reading. Anger and aggressivity were sometimes displayed in sports. The Cours Félix offered basketball. I fouled continuously and refused to pass the ball. Rugby, which was periodically played with boys on the beach, was a similar fiasco. Fencing, with its elegant, agressive movements and aristocratic roots, was reminiscent of ballet and attractive. Unfortunately the expense of the training and equipment was prohibitive. However, dear Maman persisted on weekly piano lessons, provided by an elderly spinster, Mademoiselle Rufiani. Her technique consisted of repeatedly pressing her short fingers on mine on the keys, thus accentuating certain passages of music, while simultaneously lisping and spitting out moist, stern, mispronounced admonitions "Pouthez, Mademoiselle, pouthez!" (Push, Miss, push!) instead of "Poussez!" The lady probably had some acquaintance with English, because her *s*'s sounded like an English *th*. Direct eye contact was minimized because my head was continuously averted in order to avoid the deluge. Mademoiselle told Maman that I had talent but did not study.

What else was new! I ignored Maman's remonstrances and practiced when so disposed.

Interest in boys began in class. A fifteen-year-old, young fellow with chestnut hair returned my constant stare with a smile. Invited home one day after school, for tea and cake (chaperoned by Maman, of course), he sweetly inquired whether I was "one of these Jews who wore locks and funny garments!" Shocked by the query, I cowardly denied any connection with this type of individual but never smiled at him again. My first real crush was a dark-haired, good-looking young man, a year older, who was attractive to all the girls and played hard to get. My parents reluctantly permitted me to organize a party. One boy played jazz on the piano with the top removed while accompanied by another on the banjo. François and I danced cheek to cheek to American tunes sung by Bing Crosby and other crooners of the day. The party was a blast! I hoped to be invited to other gatherings where he might be present. Noticing my silent worship, taking me aside at the end of another party, instead of an invitation for a date, smilingly, he said: "Fernande, tu es trop jeune pour moi. Quand tu auras vingt ans, promets-moi que nous nous rencontrerons sous l'Arc de Triomphe!" I was too young for him? He wanted to meet me again when I reached my twentieth birthday under the Arc of Triumph? How romantic! Ingrid Bergman and Humphrey Bogart in *Casablanca* flashed to mind. Flattered and also somewhat disappointed, in my innocence, I did not realize that François was mocking me.

The Cours Felix offered an acting competition. The literature professor thought I was perfect for the role of Racine's *Bérénice*, a Jewess, wooed by Titus, the Roman emperor. Actually, I would have preferred interpreting *Antigone* by Anouilh, which was cast with my leading rival. I won the competition with an emotional rendition prompted by the recent "lost love," emulating Edith Piaf, but with true tears. Dreams of a dramatic career then began.

France in the late forties and early fifties was exciting. I was enthralled by American jazz, as reflected in the music of Claude Luther (a French clarinetist) and the "Jazz Hot," inspired by

Sartre's existentialist philosophy with freedom of choice and responsibility for one's actions, stimulated by the feminist ideas of Simone de Beauvoir's, *The Second Sex,* found self-liberation in the rebellion of Jean Anouilh's *Antigone* and *Joan of Arc.* Descartes' precept, *Cogito ergo sum* (I think therefore I am), was discovered . . . I was intellectually clueless before my contact with Monsieur Martin, the *Professeur de Philosophie.* Good teachers are remembered. This stocky little man arrived in class wearing an eternally rumpled gray suit, with a huge dossier filled with notes, blissfully ignored, large gray mustache fluttering in the air, as he spoke. In my senior year of high school, the students were enlightened by concepts never before considered: "Where do we come from?" "Who are we?" "Where are we destined to go?" Monsieur Martin's classes were attended with enthusiasm. Introspection and control of emotions were enhanced. A poem by Alfred de Vigny called "Le Loup" (the Wolf) had great impact. Stoically, the wolf, mortally wounded, awaits death without complaint. I considered this remarkable and longed to attain this degree of self-control. In this regard, it seemed that thought analysis could be a most effective approach, and bedtime, an ideal moment to do it; which turned out to be the case.

These ideas had to be shared to be fully appreciated. Occasionally, a schoolmate and I would travel by bus to the Latin Quarter, to join a group of students sitting at Café Flore or Aux Deux Magots. Sartre's significance was among the issues discussed over a cup of café filtre, hoping to catch a glimpse of the philosopher who often visited these hangouts, with his followers. The *caves* (cellars) were also explored, to dance or listen to the music of Claude Luther or Sidney Bechet.

A career in the performing arts was not supported by my parents who desired a more practical profession particularly since high school was completed with honors. The principal of the Cours Félix acted as counselor and advised that the Hautes Etudes Commerciales (the equivalent of Harvard Business School) should be considered, in view of my records in mathematics. Since his perception of my ability in this discipline did not coincide with

my own, a combined study of politics and law was further
suggested. Totally confused, I followed the latter advice. Studies
at Sciences Politiques and Law School commenced
simultaneously. "Sciences Po" is recalled as an elite institution
in which the student body consisted chiefly of young people from
the affluent upper-middle and aristocratic classes.With little
knowledge of political and governmental affairs, this subject
matter and the school as a whole were overwhelming. English
was the only subject in which success was achieved. "Sciences
Po" was soon abandoned and replaced by concentration on Law
studies. Located in the Rue St-Jacques, the School of Law could
barely accommodate the large number of students. The professors
lecturing in the huge amphitheater, in black robe and headdress,
were scarcely known to us. Small conference groups permitted
closer direct contact with the assistant professors. The logic of
the law and its history appealed to me.

Papa was a sturdy support and studied with me. Philosophical
and political opinions were shared. He encouraged continuation
of my studies, despite my failure in the first examination.

Maman disagreed: "What do you need school? You are going
to get married and have children!"

Who thought about marriage and children? *Pas moi*! At
seventeen, I was quite innocent! The sexual act was incredulous
to me, to say the least. This was one subject not discussed with
my father! HOW COULD HE DO THAT! How humiliating!
However my curiosity was piqued, and I desired more details.
The dictionary was not helpful. For instance, "pregnancy" means
a condition of being pregnant. "Copulation" is described as a
state of being coupled. Very disappointing and frustrating! This
particular subject aside, on weekends, I would join him in the
kitchen, where usually he'd be reading Agatha Christie or
Raymond Chandler's thrillers, while Maman and Mania were still
sleeping.

My academic horizons were expanding rapidly with the
growing professional opportunities for women, and a future
career seemed assured, so I thought. Maman scoffed of course,

while Papa chuckled and reminded me teasingly of the daily Talmudic prayer which states: "Thank you Lord, for making me a man," to which my explosive disagreement was predictable. The friendly debate which followed was, nonetheless, stimulating.

*　　*　　*

Vittel in eastern France was a health spa particularly for patients with kidney disease. The "cure" consisted of hot baths, interminable massages, and drinking spring water. Listening to the band in the park's gazebo in late afternoons was an added benefit. It lasted three weeks. Maman was a faithful client. That summer, the family physician had diagnosed a "floating kidney" at my yearly physical examination, and I unwillingly accompanied Maman. To placate me, my mother authorized tennis lessons taught by a White Russian aristocrat. My progress was slow, to put it mildly. However, I did meet his son, who was my age and coincidentally also attended law school in Paris. In keeping with his social status, he took me to the horse races at the Vittel Hippodrome. While I attempted to concentrate on the spectacle which was a new and exciting experience, he continually boasted about his family royal background under the Romanoff tzars. I tried not to be impressed.

On rainy days, the French translations of *Forever Amber* and *Gone with the Wind* were voraciously read, while imbibing liters and liters of spring water (I'd never heard of "a floating kidney" but mine probably was floating, by the end of the "cure"). *Forever Amber* proved disappointing, despite being forbidden and supposedly very "sexy." Even the dictionary previously consulted had been more helpful. *Gone with the Wind* was something else entirely. Scarlett, the Civil War survivor, became my ideal of womanhood. Her rebellion against the establishment, attachment to the land, and belief that "tomorrow is another day" were incorporated in my modus vivendi. The movie was released in France in 1949, and the family joined the long lines of people desiring to see it. Would Rhett Butler's final famous line, "Frankly my dear, I don't give a damn!" from the book be replaced, in the film, by the usual final sweet Hollywood kiss? Helas, no! . . . The cinema continued to be our prime source of entertainment. Subtle French war films such as Marcel Carné's *Visiteurs du Soir,* with its allusions to Vichy, and *Les Enfants du Paradis* were admirable. I cried with Micheline Presle in *Boule de Suif* and *Paradis Perdu* which dealt with World War I. American war films in particular, far less subtle psychologically, were enthusiastically cheered whenever the Germans were inevitably defeated. Ambition for dramatic career returned. I debated whether to become a lawyer or a movie star. Dreadful stories concerning Hollywood and the possibility of losing your virginity on a director's couch were discouraging. During the hour bus trip to Rue St-Jacques, there was time to fantasize meeting Gary Grant, Gary Cooper, and Gregory Peck. However, parental encouragement was absent and my ambition and determination insufficient. This dream soon dissipated. Resigned, I returned to the study of law and discussions with Papa.

During adolescence, my *Yiddishe Momme* was fiercely resented. *She annoys me. Her Jewishness annoys me. Her false teeth annoy me. The other day she slapped me because I did not admire her taste in clothes. "Don't hit me! I am fifteen."* She answered, *"Ich ver dir gibben a frask afem pisk wen ich vill. Ich bin dine mutter"* (I'll hit you when I want, I am your mother). *Why do I have to sleep with her while Papa is in the beautiful new room furnished for me? Why does she have to prepare a hope-chest when she knows I do not want to get married? Besides, who is this "schmuck" (she calls him that) named Motzali who regularly sells those gorgeous linens for a trousseau which is not wanted? She plays the grande dame with Emilienne, our young maid, a paysanne from Brittany. Maman sits at the head of the table, talking to our guests. Suddenly, she vigorously shakes the tiny bell near her plate and is ignored. The bell is shaken once again. Silence. After the third attempt, Maman yells at the top of her voice, "Emiiiiiii . . . lieeeeee . . . nne!" Emilienne comes in, shuffling in slippers, and sullenly murmurs,"Ouai! Quoi?"*

(Yeah! What?). *Maman's efforts at playing the grande dame are in vain.*

Maman referred to me as a *schlang* (a snake), and with good reason. Believing her fasting and nonsmoking on Yom Kippur were hypocritical, I ATE.

My mother's atrocious French was spoken with a pronounced Yiddish accent and very poor grammar that caused me to cringe with shame. My school chums mocked the accent. How could my mother speak like that! One day, when I was sixteen, on exiting a fine boutique on the Champs-Elysées, she said, "Dir gefellt wus mir hobben gekoyft?"(Do you like what we bought?) Sacrilège! Yiddish on the Champs-Elysées? Maman had dared desecrate the French language and, compounding the cruel felony, had the temerity to speak Yiddish on this illustrious avenue? Henri IV's assassin had been drawn and quartered for the murder of the French sovereign. But did she deserve the same fate?

"Don't speak Yiddish on the Champs-Elysées," I said with hauteur, walking quickly away. Maman was unfazed. To my utter embarrassment, she loudly yelled, "Antisemitke!" Indeed!

Another requirement, under duress, was attendence at Yiddish theater. On one such evening, the great actor Maurice Schwartz performed in *The Dybbuk* (a play written by Shlomo Rapaport—S-Anski) at the theater Sarah Bernhardt. I despised the noisy audience, Maman, and the play. Yiddish was spoken throughout the theater. But *moi*, who studied Molière and Voltaire, had to endure this vulgar tongue!

However, this story of mysticism was fascinating, although never publicly acknowledged. The deceased lover who possesses the soul of his bride, betrothed to another man, appealed to my sense of the romantic.

Please forgive me, Maman. This anti-Semitic rebellion resulted in feasting on Yom Kippur while you fasted, lying prostrate in bed with a fierce headache and dating Catholic boys, gleefully promising to marry one.

Despite the rebellion, force of habit causes me to continue sleeping with my mother. This pattern has to change and results in a decision to sleep alone in *my* room! . . . The initial nights, usually awake, are extremely difficult, punctuated by Maman's visits to see if my determination has weakened. *It has not.* The temptation to join my parents is great. *I do not.* It is the first significant step towards personal freedom and adulthood.

Florette remains my confidante for a while. Sometimes we meet along the Seine, browsing the *bouquinistes* (bookstands), seeking a certain antique book or particular poster at reasonable price. While on vacation in Juan-les-Pins, we secretly share our first cigarette in the bathroom, and nearly choke. During a Christmas holiday in 1949, tiring and discouraging ski lessons are abandoned and replaced by the pleasures of belote in the cozy hotelroom in Megève. However, school keeps us busy; we have different friends and interests and finally have gone our separate ways.

Most often, I am alone, often confused and angry.

Now, I am remorseful.

War, intolerance, fear, and hatred were experienced at an early age. The events occurred without full comprehension on my part, and without evident sympathy or empathy from those around me, except from my loving parents. I reacted primarily to matters of survival. Back in Paris, in the post-war years of the late 1940s and '50s, I was a confused teenager, timid, innocent, resentful of the recent past and uncertain future. I was slowly maturing, accepting paternal encouragement, rejecting maternal overprotectiveness, and awakening to the knowledge acquired in books, school, and personal relationships. However, it has taken fifty years to come to terms with the experiences of early childhood.

# CHAPTER XV

## SEARCH FOR IDENTITY

... And then, I discover Israël.

In 1946, cousin Sigi, now a handsome young man in his early twenties, arrives from Palestine. Sigi is very enthusiastic about a future Jewish state and looks dashing in a British Army uniform. He is to be married (*hélas*! I have a crush on him) in Brussels. The family is invited to the wedding. Afterwards, the young couple will leave for Palestine. Papa's sister, Rosa, and her husband Isaac will join them.

Two years later, Ben Gurion emotionally announces the establishment of the Jewish state. Israël is immediately recognized by President Harry S. Truman, on behalf of the United States of America.

In 1949, Papa has a surprise for my seventeenth birthday. Maman and I shall visit Israël. It is the first anniversary of the Jewish state's independence. There will be a great celebration in Tel-Aviv. Theodor Herzl's body is to be brought from Vienna for reinterment in *Eretz Israël*.

School ends in July, but first, it is necessary to pass the baccalauréat examination. Then, *Vive les Vacances*! (Hurrah for the vacation!) In the meantime, I take Hebrew lessons, but only learn to say, "Ani lo medaberet Ivrit" (I don't speak Hebrew). Our departure is marred by my failure to pass the written part of the baccalauréat. It has to be repeated in October. This examination is so difficult that I am subject to recurring nightmares. Some students commit suicide. This contretemps could, no doubt, spoil the trip.

Once onboard ship, these bad moments are forgotten. The voyage to Israël is joyous. Maman and I have an outside cabin on the *Mare Ligure*, a five-thousand-ton Italian vessel. Passengers, including Maman, are seasick. Some sailors and the ship's doctor do not fare so well either. A set of false teeth are vomited overboard! The few able to enjoy the food and entertainment include myself, a few other youths, and a handsome young Italian midshipman who shamelessly flirts with me. Neither he nor I speak the other's language. Glances are exchanged. We dance the *Hora* with our small group on the bridge and sleep on the deck in lounge chairs, while poor Maman and other passengers suffer below. The travelers gather on the bow of the ship on arrival in Haifa. It is a very poignant moment. People cry as they first glimpse *Eretz Israël*. Some passengers kiss the ground after disembarking. The experience has so much meaning after all the suffering. "The Passover meal ends with 'Next year in Jerusalem,'" says Maman, exhausted from the trip, and joyously yells out, "We made it!"

Gazing at the security guards, soldiers, the customs officials, and the milling crowd of shouting people of all ages, suddenly, I am struck by the proud realization that "Everyone is Jewish! How about that!"

This feeling of exhilaration remains during the entire two months. Jerusalem is visited.

The Mandelbaum Gate (50) is situated near the Mea Shearim district, which is inhabited by ultraorthodox Jews. Our guide takes us to the roof of an apartment building near the gate but directs that extreme caution be exerted while peeping over the parapet, to avoid being shot by Jordanian snipers, not too distant on the other side. Watching the news on television nowadays, things have hardly changed! Snipers have been replaced by homicide bombers.

Paradoxically, at the end of the excursion, it becomes

necessary to hurry to the taxi. I am pursued by ultraorthodox children who throw stones and yell "whore" in Hebrew because my shoulders and midriff are bared in a summer outfit, which is prohibited, according to their tradition. This totally unexpected discrimination and abuse from my own people are never forgotten. It is too reminiscent of the young Yennois, who also threw rocks and called me, *sale youpine!*

Sigi and Mickey, with their newborn baby girl Mira, invite us to share their small white stone house in Ramat-Yitzrak, a little town near Tel-Aviv, surrounded by desert sand. During the day, oranges are picked in the nearby orchard and stored in the bathtub. Coyotes howl at night, beneath the windows. Sigi and Mickey are young, amusing, and a joy to accompany to Tel-Aviv in the evenings, to dance in the seaside cafés. It is pleasing that Maman has forgiven Isaac. Family dinners with him and Aunt Rosa become routine.

Maman has relatives in Kibbutz Afikim, near the Golan Heights. (During a later visit, it is discovered that the Syrians regularly shelled the kibbutz area, before the Israëlis took the Heights during the Six-Day War in 1967.) Abraham, Mania's nephew, and his family, graciously receive us. During the work week, the small children of the kibbutz are cared for by the female members, who are trained and assigned to this task. This arrangement permits the parents to work in the fields, farms, or factory within the compound, their minds at ease. In the evening, the children return home.

An invitation to a kibbutz wedding is received. The bride and groom, as well as the guests, are dressed simply, in sharp contrast with the formal attire usually worn at Jewish weddings in France. A single harmonica player leads the lively singing and dancing with the joyous encouragement of the guests and shouts of "Mazel Tov! Mazel Tov!" There is no hired professional band. The music was of the kibbutz and the Middle East, but not the *shtetl.*

One daily activity I intensely disliked was the siesta, which occurred during the midday hours, when the sun is at its zenith and hottest. *It was boring.* Only illness could cause me to sleep in the afternoon. I attempted to read. However my relatives took this "snooze" in a common room, with a lonely fan. There are no spare rooms in a kibbutz. Unfortunately, the only way to escape the snores was outside in the extreme heat of day, which is where I usually went, looking for a shady spot, often without success, until 3:00 PM when the *kibbutzniks* returned to work or other activities. While in Tel-Aviv, the siesta was also ignored, and on one occasion, I decided to walk on Dizengoff Boulevard, despite dire warnings to the contrary. The sun was scorchingly hot, the pavement burning underfoot, and the street deserted. This outdoor furnace was endured for a long ten minutes whereupon I retreated to the stone house with its cool tiled floors.

We learned Hebrew songs, viewed an old Eddie Cantor film, and swam in the *Kinneret* (the Sea of Galilee). Exotic foods such as *Falafel* (spicy vegetable dumpling), *Hummus* (ground chickpeas), and corn on the cob (in France, only farm animals eat corn) were sampled. A performance of Shakespeare's *Midsummer Night's Dream,* in Hebrew, was seen at a theater in Tel-Aviv. Although the language was mostly incomprehensible, the play was enjoyed anyway, since the story plot was so well known. The creative movements of the actors appeared balletic.

These many activities and experiences made this voyage unforgettable.

The Israëlis' idealism, enthusiasm, and love of country are most impressive and touching.

Armed soldiers are everywhere. Many of these young men and women, born in Israël, are tall, blond, tan, and good looking. They are called *Sabras*, a fruit outwardly tough but soft and tender within. How ironic! Scarcely the image of the *Juif Süss*!

Frustrated, unable to communicate in French, English, or German, I finally murmur, in desperation, "Yiddish?" This young *antisemitke* is astonished to converse in *Mammeloschen* (mother tongue) for the first time.

The older generation wants me to remain in Israël. I have little in common with the new immigrants, many of whom are concentration camp survivors or refugees from other countries. Yad Vachem (51) does not exist as yet. The Holocaust is not a popular topic for conversation.

The survivors are considered weak, pitiful people and led like sheep to the gas chambers without resisting.

Now, Israelis are fighters.

"Young people are needed here!"

"But I want to return to France, to Paris, to Papa, and to my studies!"

"Promise you will come back."

"I promise."

Return I did, after many years, with my family.

The ship for France awaited us in Haifa, to which we took a bus from Tel-Aviv. At the depot, I needed a pen to record an address. A Hassid, dressed in black, with a fur hat, seemed a reasonable person to ask for assistance in Yiddish. He extended the pen in my direction but averted his face. Affronted, I questioned Maman as to the reason. Apparently ultraorthodox Jewish men do not look directly at women (to preclude temptation of the flesh). Till then, I was unaware that there were significantly different "types of Jews!" molded by vastly varied cultural, ethnic, racial, religious, and historic backgrounds. My own identity was gradually taking shape.

The Israeli ship returning to Marseille was filled with young European men who had fought in the Hagganah during Israel's War of Independence in 1947–1948. There was an Englishman with a cockney accent, with whom I practiced my rudimentary English. He described White Chapel, then a predominently Jewish area in London's East End where his parents resided.

The objective of this visit to Israël was attained. Back in Paris, I was a radically changed individual who had discovered Zionism and no longer an anti-Semite. Papa bought a large silver *Mogen David* (Star of David) for me, which was as ostentatiously displayed as the Crosses of my friends. Still uncomfortable as a Jew in France, I nevertheless now flaunted it.

Papa had purchased a Citroën *Traction Avant* and invited a

friend who had experience with this vehicle to take a drive in the country. Paul was at the wheel, with Father in the adjacent front seat. At the top of a hill, coming in the opposite direction, a truck with a drunken driver, struck the Citroën head-on . . . Paul died on impact. Papa survived with a broken nose, arm, and leg but could not speak, so enveloped with bandages that his clinical status appeared worse than it actually was. On returning from the hospital, Maman succumbed to the situation with pitiful sobs, fearing my father's demise. She sat in a chair, a tear-soaked handkerchief crushed in hand . . . Suddenly adult, I knelt before my mother, took her cold hands in mine, and soothingly comforted her. What would happen if Papa died? Times were bad in France; the shoe factory faced heavy taxation. I very firmly told her that he would survive, that we would survive, and I would help her deal with the family financial responsibilities during papa's convalescence.She appeared relieved. Papa recovered.

On a sadder note, the suspicions concerning my father's affair with Mania were reinforced. Maman had turned a blind eye during these past years but, on the return from Israël, made me a reluctant confidante. Loathing Mania, I continued to adore Papa and sought an excuse for this behavior. Now that I was old enough to understand, it was difficult to reconcile his infidelity with my love for him.

"It's your fault!" I told my mother. "Why did you leave him alone with her and take me on vacation? *La chair est faible* (flesh is weak)," I added. "It was a temptation, and he was not strong enough to resist."

"But how could he?" cried my mother. "I trusted him."

Torn between the two, I was unable to influence the situation. At that time, there was no question of divorce, since my parents considered the family unit essential for my welfare. The problem resolved itself regrettably after Mania suffered a stroke, resulting in partial paralysis and loss of speech. (Some years later, she immigrated to Israël with the help of Abraham, her nephew.)

On the Israeli ship, returning to France, I met a young French Jew, Ralph, who had volunteered in the *Hagganah*. After a few months, I was introduced to his parents, who were concentration camp survivors, now journalists. They were intellectuals, which impressed me. I was influenced by Ralph's Zionism. His father had written a book concerning World War II experiences, of which I have a copy. During the war, Ralph and Marc, his five-year-old brother, were sheltered in an orphanage in the Dordogne (a province in southwest France). Their parents instructed their sons to meet them in Strasbourg at the end of the hostilities. The boys escaped the orphanage at the end of the war, traversing France to Strasbourg by foot, where, unbelievably, they located their parents! Ralph wanted to marry me but lacked a formal education and a job, while I was very motivated by my studies.

Israël: in Kibbutz Affikim with Aunt Rosa near me,
Abraham, and Bunia (left)
(Mania's nephew and niece)

Uncle Isaac, Aunt Rosa, and their son Sami

My cousin Sigi

The romance ended; Ralph went to Germany and, fluent in the language, also became a journalist with the help of his father.

My mother had made it clear that virginity was mandatory for a girl until marriage. Nothing could be more repugnant than a single, pregnant young woman, which really was stressful. During the second year of law school, Maman decided to make a *schidech*. My apparent disinterest in men was actually shyness. Books and studies were preferable and safe, because they did not depend on personal relationships. Judaism remained a constant problem; anti-Semitic remarks were frequent, but now, they were responded to aggressively.

I disliked my reflection in the mirror which paradoxically was manifested by a lack of interest in clothes or appearance. This worried Maman. She bought me fashionable dresses, and eligible young Jewish men were introduced . . . Most girls in school smoked. At parties, it was "cool" to hold a cigarette in one hand and a drink in the other. In order to attract attention and hide my insecurity at the same time, my response to an offer of cigarettes, at such parties, was invariably: "Non, merci, je ne fume pas!" Boys were surprised by my refusal. They invited me to dance but nothing further. My conversation was apparently uninteresting, and after a while, I was ignored. Were they boring or was I? Perhaps both. A young man invited me to see Walt Disney's *Fantasia*. Afterwards, over coffee, I recall being insecure and unworthy during his monologue on physics, and Vivaldi, since I was quite ignorant of both. My silence was so deafening that he never asked me out again, happily, as it turned out. Next time, I was determined to be more knowledgeable concerning music if not physics!

Although English was not offered in law school, I continued to read books written in that language, spending a summer in Wales with a pen pal. This was a great summer; English, especially with a Welsh accent, was quite a challenge.The Welsh family took me to the beach in Aberystwyth. I learned cricket, taught them to sing: "Alouette . . . gentille alouette!" and discovered plum pudding and high tea. However, there was no opportunity to meet eligible Jewish boys.

In desperation, my mother sent me to the United States in 1952, to cousins Betty and Henry for the ultimate catch: a rich, handsome young American Jewish doctor. It was a difficult decision for Maman, allowing me to travel alone, but Papa insisted. The trip to Israel had been a maturing experience.

This was my first voyage on a French ship, the *Ile de France*, and I shyly remained in the cabin, leaving it only for meals, movies, and the final ball where I met an attractive young American man. I refused a cigarette but danced with him for most of the evening. Finally, he sheepishly admitted studying for the priesthood. My luck!

The summer with my relatives was a great disappointment. Their tight restrictions and constant nagging inhibited my ability to become more knowledgeable about the United States. However, I met some wonderful people, in particular, my dear, now-departed friend Isabel who was like an older sister. After visiting the White House, she introduced me to Maryland University, football, and a group of interesting young American students and arranged a party in my honor, in New York. French and American songs were sung, accompanied by one of the guests at the piano. My rendition of *The Cancan* fulfilled the American audience's common perception of a French stereotype.

Near the end of my stay in New York City, on Rosh Hashanah Eve, I had promised to meet my relatives at the synagogue in Washington Heights after a picnic with friends. Rebellious as usual, I arrived home late. They had already left for services. *No problem! I'll enquire where the synagogue is located.* In the street, a man with a *yarmulke* (skullcap) and a prayer book approached. "Please, sir, could you tell me where the synagogue is?"

He said, "Which one?"

"How many synagogues do you have?" I replied, smiling, remembering that Paris has about three or four large synagogues, but in separate districts.

"There are quite a few in the neighborhood."

After receiving directions, I went searching for my cousins and finally found them in the sixth temple! The services by then were almost finished, for which I was very grateful!

The large number of Jews in New York City and in Israël was truly amazing! I realized that my world was no longer dominated by French Catholics. Discovering the United States was a unique experience, with long-lasting, profound effects.

Betty and Henry, in response to Maman's desperate request to find an American husband, diligently obliged, and soon I was introduced to several eligible bachelors, but without result. Determined to return to the family in France, and a career, my cousins, to their chagrin, considered me a "spoiled brat" and unworthy of their prospective suitors. They perhaps were right. My feminist and socialist ideals shocked them. It was the McCarthy era, and they were afraid to voice their opinion. After the wartime experiences, this fearful attitude was incomprehensible. At times, simply to express independence and annoyance with their outlook, I would sing the communist's "international" anthem and drink wine or beer instead of milk. It was mutual culture shock. They were glad to be rid of me. On the last night in New York, I met charming Mickey K, who, with an orchid corsage in hand and profound intellectual conversation, tried to persuade me to remain in the States and marry him! It was tempting. But fate had other plans, and I only promised to write.

The voyage on the *Ile de France* to America took nine days and was considered too long after an absence of two months. My ticket was exchanged for travel on the SS *United States*, which crossed in five days. A cabin was shared with three other women: a New York widow, a Southern belle named Delilah, and a young woman my age, Ellen, on her way to Switzerland to continue her studies. Ellen persuaded me to meet a group of American medical students on their way back to Heidelberg, Germany, who were traveling in economy class. The "Love Boat" existed for me long before the television show. This is where I met my future husband Edward. It was not love at first sight. Ellen had her eye on Edward, but so did I. Since he did not show any apparent interest in me, I flirted with one of his schoolmates. The time on board ship passed quickly.

My shyness diminished in response to the easy company, music, and interesting conversation. One evening, we gathered around a table in the cabaret. The wine was relaxing, and I sang a French song, "La Vie en Rose." Edward laughed at an attempted imitation of my favorite vocalist, Edith Piaf. I was glowing, having finally attracted his attention, and encouraged, I further entertained him with a repertoire of Jewish songs (thank you, Maman), particularly:

"Hot ha Yid ha weibbele." (A Jew has a little wife.)
"Hot ha Yid tsurres." (A Jew has a lot of trouble.)
"Hot ha Yid ha weibbele." (A Jew has a little wife.)
"Oy, toyg sie auf kapores." (Aye, she is good for nothing.)

Edward understood Yiddish. He was twenty-two years old and had brown hair and high forehead and cheekbones. Rugged in appearance, he moved like an athlete, fluid and graceful. I thought him pleasing to the eye. I fell in love with his laughing hazel eyes and crooked front teeth, partly revealed when smiling. A very quiet young man with a wry sense of humor, who laughed heartily at his friends' antics, could also be serious when discussing politics. After walking around the deck, we sat on lounge chairs, exchanging thoughts about his studies and my war experiences. It was decided we meet in Paris. The news of Eisenhower's election to the presidency greeted us on arriving in Le Havre the next day.

Eddy and his friends came to my home where Maman frantically prepared *latkes* (potato pancakes) for dinner. Later that night, I accompanied my new friends to the train station. Eddy and I held hands and gazed at each other, promising to write. We had our first kiss on the quay of the Gare de l'Est. This was the beginning of our courtship and our fifty years together.

Eddy came back at Christmas and proposed. Maman was in

seventh heaven and exclaimed, "Gevalt! A Yiddischer Yingel!" (My goodness! A Jewish boy!) So was I.

We introduced him to our entourage. Eddy did not know any French and was quiet. Maman's girlfriends ogled him, smiled, and repeatedly insisted that "he was very handsome but extremely quiet." Tata Jeannette invited the whole family to her apartment, and Eddy became acquainted with endless French-Jewish luncheons. Tonton Jean worriedly kept on saying to me: "Traduis-lui! Traduis-lui!" (Translate for him! Translate for him!) Ed was having a good time, having imbibed all sorts of wine and liqueurs and was regaled by Tonton Jean's famous "sur la pointe des pieds" (on your tippitoes). He had to kiss cheeks, shake innumerable hands and, by the late afternoon, whispered in my ear that he longed to take a walk. Out of the question! We were on our way to Tata Fanny for dinner and a repeat performance.

My American fiancé insisted on comparing the beautiful Champs-Elysées to the "beautiful" Grand Concourse in the Bronx, New York. I was offended, and it behooved me to "educate" him. I dragged him, complaining to the ballet to see The Marquis de Cuevas Ballet Company in Stravinsky's *Petrushka*. Eddy eventually became an aficionado. The usual tourist attractions including the Louvre were visited. Marc, now a champion at saber, invited us to observe a fencing exhibition in his high school. The Haitian master-at-arms permitted Eddy to take a brief lesson in épée, which proved thoroughly enjoyable.

Eddy thought that the temple where the ceremony would take place was *progressive* or *reformed*. He had been brought up in the *conservative* tradition. *What was this all about?* A loud argument ensued because I neither knew nor cared about the differences, whereupon the temper of my future husband was first encountered . . .

"What do you mean you don't care? The children must be raised as Jews."

"I don't care about religion!"

"If you don't care about religion, then you are not a Jew!"

This comment was unacceptable.

"I am as good a Jew as you are. I have suffered enough during the war to know."

That stopped him. Disagreements, no matter how sharply defined, should not cause permanent rift in a relationship, provided the "combatants" have sufficient respect and affection for each other, as was the case in this and similar conflicts. For example, I never kept a kosher home because it had no importance for me, although it certainly was a necessity for my future mother-in-law.

Ed's parents and friends came to the wedding in Paris. France requires a civil ceremony prior to the religious rite, according to the Napoleonic Code. This was performed by the mayor of Levallois, a tricolor sash arrayed across his chest, at the city hall, and naturally carried out in French. Eddy did not understand the language. I would nudge him at the appropriate moment to respond with "oui." One question, however, concerning a marriage contract required a "non" but almost received the incorrect response. After some confusion and much laughter, we finally got it straight. The religious service was scheduled for the next day.

The synagogue, one of the oldest in Paris, whose construction commenced in 1819, is still designated as the Rue Notre-Dame-de-Nazareth Temple. Eddy was not exactly sure of its location, was even more confused by its name which seemed incongruous, and therefore, reluctant to give the proper address to the taxidriver, got lost. In the interim, my beautiful floral bouquet was wilting in the summer heat (no air-conditioning in those days). When he finally arrived at the temple door, I burst out laughing at his dishevelled appearance in morning clothes and top hat. Maman's sobs of joy accompanied the cantor's falsetto. The beautiful Hebraic hymns were projected along with a prolific, fine, moist spray, which was difficult to avoid given the limited space under the *Chuppah* (wedding canopy). Our continous giggling was fortunately eclipsed by the reverential stentorian chants.

Lutetia is the Latin name for Paris and means the City of Lights. The reception took place at the Hotel Lutetia, the locale of many weddings of upper-middle-class Jewish families. The affair proved to be a huge success.

Our parents got along famously. Language was not a problem. They conversed in Yiddish. It was amazing that Jews from different countries were able to communicate in one of the universal languages of the Jewish people, the other being Ladino. The mothers, while shopping, learned snippets of each other's native tongue, mixing Yiddish with either English or French, depending on the occasion. For instance Maman said to my mother-in-law: "Minnie, es regent, mir namen *un parapluie*" (Minnie, it rains, let's take *an umbrella*). Minnie, at the end of a meal, offered: "Mir machen *the dishes* zusammen" (we do the *dishes* together). My father-in-law and Maman, of similar temperament, really enjoyed bantering with one another.

One thing was sure. Maman almost had her dream come true: she caught a handsome young Jewish American medical student (not rich) as a son-in-law.

# CHAPTER XVI

## JE SUIS BIEN DANS MA PEAU

It is virtually an impossible task to recount fifty years of a marriage in these relatively few pages. I'll not attempt it. Our life had its ups and downs but has been productive, rewarding and comfortable, overall. My husband completed his studies and became a physician. We raised a family. Our children enjoyed childhood and adolescence in a moderately affluent small community in northern New Jersey, with few Jewish families. Although religious rituals remained unappealing to me, celebrating traditions such as Passover, Chanukah, Rosh Hashanah, and Yom Kippur were important because it reaffirmed our identity, giving the children a sense of belonging which had been absent in my early life. Being Jewish in the United States was so different than in France, where assimilation was the norm. This was facilitated by the educational system and the state.

With multiculturalism prevalent in France, things are changing nowadays, but slowly. The French are very uncomfortable with Muslims unwilling to abandon their traditions. My parents and many other Jews of their generation had no such compunction. It did not prevent discrimination, however. Most fortunately, my children experienced very little of the fear, hatred, and bigotry characteristic of my youth. When Deborah was in first grade, I sent a note of thanks to her teacher for having a Chanukah menorah next to the Christmas tree. When Marc encountered anti-Semitic comments from a "friend," my liberating response to the mother by phone was, "You don't have to love me, but you'll have to tolerate me!" Such an answer was unimaginable in France before or even after the war. Now too, probably, given the vicious anti-Semitism prevalent in my country of birth.

After the children were old enough to attend school, I returned to the university, eventually receiving a bachelor of arts degree then a master of arts in teaching, which permitted me to become an instructor at the Academy of the Holy Angels, which was my home away from home for twenty-four years. At this school, my Jewish identity was further reinforced. For the first time in my life I was respected as a Jew and quite at ease, since my youth had been spent among Catholics. Deborah, my oldest child, graduated from the academy. Teaching colleagues jokingly would say, "Fernande, you'll never get fired. You are the school's token Jew, and besides, you are French!" In fact, over the years, there have been several Jewish teachers and employees at this institution. Here, I was able to blossom personally and professionally. Once a year, at the anniversary of *Kristallnacht*, I was asked to explain the terrible actions of the Nazis during that "Night of The Broken Glass" to the students and the staff at morning announcements. A Passover model *"Seder"* was offered to students. The History Department requested that I discuss my memories of World War II in France. On the first such occasion, both the class and I burst into tears. However, it is necessary that both young and old be periodically reminded of these events.

Madame Moliaix's principles and heroism were never forgotten; teaching tolerance became part of my curriculum.

\*    \*    \*

Nowadays, with the responsibilities and concerns of daily life, I scarcely reflect on the loss of my beloved parents, long gone. The memories are simply too painful. When we first parted, after my marriage, so many years ago, I must admit, perhaps with some guilt, to a unique sense of freedom and joy I'd never before experienced. There was no longer anyone to direct my life, except my husband who tried, but usually without effect. Marriages tend to be more successful, particularly early on, without parental interference however well meant, and enhances one's own responsibility. This was facilitated since they lived far away.

My mother had been ill for some time, her condition deteriorating, and she was to be hospitalized for congestive heart failure. That afternoon, she pitifully cried: "Eddale, Eddale!" calling my husband for help. Eddy could do no wrong at least in my mother's eyes, since he cared for Papa, following a heart attack, some years before. Maman was moaning, had difficulty in breathing, and was quite agitated. I stood helplessly at her bedside, holding her hand, paralyzed by deep anxiety, bathed in a cold sweat. Grimly, Eddy and my father followed the stretcher to the ambulance, then drove to the hospital. I remained behind with Deborah who was only seven months old. Eddy returned that evening and took me to see Maman. I was only permitted a brief glance into the hospital room, through which I could see little of my mother, save an oxygen tent and plastic tubing in her nose and arms. *Could this be my maman who had been so full of life? It could not be true. Time would revert, and things would go on as before.* She had been ill for so long a period that the possibility of impending death seemed so remote. I was unprepared.

She passed away that night, and the interment was equally as quick, as prescribed in the Jewish faith. Maman was fifty-eight years old. The finite image, which I have been unable to erase, is her coffin being lowered neither gracefully nor too gently into the ground. My sanity, in the ensuing days and months, was only preserved by Deborah's joyous laughter and mischief.

It was also during this time that our second child was conceived. Amniocentesis had not as yet been developed, and Eddy and I were looking forward to the birth of either a healthy girl or boy. However, after delivery, physically fatigued and emotionally drained, I burst into tears upon discovering that the baby was a girl. The obstetrician inquired whether I was disappointed.

"Not at all, to the contrary," I replied sniffing, "I am delighted to have a daughter who will be named Vera in honor of my mother."

Papa remarried a year later. He was lonely, and this concerned me. His new wife, Helen, a widow who had spent the war years hidden in Paris, took very good care of Papa, and they appeared happy together. Papa and I understood each other. As we aged, our friendship grew. I have always had a profound love and admiration for my father who, after leaving Poland, repeatedly had to commence life again, first in Germany, then France, Canada, and finally the United States. Papa, the eternal optimist, never gave up. Since I was not yet an American citizen, he was unable to immigrate immediately to the United States. Instead he came to Canada with Maman, learned English, and returned to his former trade: leathercutting. Papa was no longer the "patron" but simply a factory worker again. He never complained. Maman could not forget the days of Madame Henri (wife of the *Patron*) with the privilege of money, furs, and jewels. The geographic translocations and the diminished socioeconomic status was the onset of her decline. Papa, the tough, independent, self-made man, to the contrary, was a survivor. I remember his visits prior his remarriage. Quietly, he would wake up early and prepare breakfast for himself. As before, he'd be sitting in the kitchen, enjoying toast with cheese and coffee while reading a detective story, his favorite pastime. Still my confidant, he would listen as usual to my hopes and concerns and advise me wisely. In the middle of a hot July night, Helen telephoned in panic. Papa had another heart attack. Reluctantly I had to remain at home with the three children. Eddy rushed to Brooklyn as I worriedly paced the bedroom, fearing the worst. Papa died that night. The funeral took place the following day. I could not mourn and wondered why. My father, whom I loved so dearly, had passed, and yet I had no tears. About a year later, suddenly overcome by the full realization of my loss, release finally came, and I wept.

Cancer struck in the 1980s. The experience was frightening, debilitating, disfiguring, and depressing. While fortunate to have the support of my husband and children, it was, nevertheless, a lonely trial. Five of my closest friends perished from this dreadful disease. Years passed before I was emotionally able to accept what had occurred. An incidental visit helped me cope with it. After Papa's death, his second wife, Helen, remarried a concentration camp survivor and later invited our little family to a Sunday lunch. The facial expressions of the children, when shown her husband's striped concentration camp uniform, were unforgettable; so was her husband's comment, "I keep this to remind myself to do what I want, while I still can, and fear nothing." This is an application of *Carpe Diem* (seize the day). It governs my daily life, just as it had my father's.

This disease was another turning point. The cocoon in which I had slowly matured was now gone. The caterpillar had finally become a butterfly. I was *bien dans ma peau* (feeling good in my skin). Montaigne, a sixteenth-century French philosopher and politician, who, lacking control of political and personal events, accepted what could not be changed, as described in his memoir, the *Essais*. After reading it, so did I. The rigidity and control, with which my children were burdened, gradually diminished. They were free to determine their own destiny.

For many years I did not consider myself a Holocaust survivor. The victims of the concentration and forced-labor camps, whose horrific experiences were memorialized in articles, books, photographs, or in films, were the only true survivors. Eventually, I began to realize, although our respective histories differered radically, that we shared collectively the cause of that "Reign of Terror." Stated simply and directly, the murderous, unadorned hatred of the Jewish people. Therefore, I too was a survivor.

According to Simone Veil, members of the Resistence, who returned from imprisonment in Germany, were honored while Jews coming back from the concentration camps felt rejected since their presence was troublesome to people. (52) I did not wish to discuss these war memories. It had been a traumatic period, and best forgotten. Reluctantly when I spoke of it, the apparent interest of the listeners was surprising, "Fernande, you must write about this . . ." At first, their query was not easily understandable since my experiences paled, compared to those from the camps.

The Holocaust has become an event of enormous historic interest. Numerous scholarly texts continue to be published. Holocaust studies have been developed in high school and university curricula. Museums and memorials have been dedicated to recalling this terrible chapter, particularly throughout Europe and the United States. The memories were so dreadful. It was easier to revisit other historic tragedies, such as the centuries-old conflict in Ireland or even the Spanish Inquisition. How long could I ignore the past?

I began to consider putting my memories to paper.

Some years ago, my family persuaded me to view *Au-Revoir, les Enfants*, a film by Louis Malle. Near the movie's end, Jean Bonnet (alias Kippelstein) follows Père Jean as he leaves the school grounds on the way to Auschwitz. The very last image of the narrator Julien (Louis Malle), who is witness to Père Jean's arrest by the Nazis for harboring Jewish children, is devastating as he states, "I'll never forget this day until I die."

Holocaust films such as *Shoah*, *Hotel Terminus*, *Schindler's List*, and *The Pianist* were also difficult to watch. However, the documentary which perhaps was most affecting as a French native is *The Sorrow and the Pity*, which revealed the complicity and perfidy of the French during World War II. Understandably, the French did not wish to acknowledge this complicity. At first the film could only be seen at private screenings primarily in the United States but not in France. Although I was fully aware of Vichy's collaboration, it was nevertheless shocking to hear the callous and indifferent remarks made by some of the participants interviewed. My feelings were ambivalent. How was I to deal with my Jewishness, vis-à-vis the love-hate relationship for France?

Several pilgrimages to Yenne proved helpful. On walking through the streets, André Chagnon and Adrienne Lenoir reintroduced me to passersby, café *patrons* (bosses), the postman, and store owners who remembered my family. Handshakes and smiles of greeting were exchanged. Were these the same people who had ignored us, thrown stones, or expressed hatred in some fashion or another? Suddenly, everyone appeared friendly!

Tante Marie, Michèle's aunt, invited us and other townspeople, who had known my family, to her garden. It was a hot summer afternoon, and the group was seated in the tree-shaded backyard, cool drinks in hand. To celebrate, bottles of champagne were also opened. Conversation was lively, recalling past occasions:

"Tu étais très élégante!" (You were very elegant!)
"Ah oui? Pourquoi?" (Yes? Why?)
"Tu portais toujours des gants!" (You always wore gloves!)

I asked what they thought of Jean-Marie le Pen, the ultra right-wing politician who opposes immigration, particularly by the Arabs. Did they think anti-Semitism was on the rise in France?

"Il est dangereux!" said one guest.

André shook his head, "Moi, pourvu qu'on ne m'emmerde pas, ça m'est égal, juif ou arabe" (Me, as long as nobody bothers me, I don't care, Jew or Arab).

What do young people think of the Holocaust? "C'était tellement inhumain, c'est comme un film. Les jeunes ne sont pas sensibles à la question. Ils en sont fatigués, comme nous l'étions par la guerre de 14-18." (It was so inhuman, it's like a film. The youth are not sensitive to the question. They are tired of it just as we were fed up with stories of World War I).

Recollections of Sunday mornings around the breakfast table

with Deborah, Vera, and Marc-David, in their pajamas, come fondly to mind. Noisy conversation was interrupted by the solemn voice of their father, declaring that the lesson in Jewish history was about to commence. Their sullen faces portrayed a mix of somnolence and extreme lack of enthusiasm. Were they actually listening or thinking about friends, parties, and ball games? It nevertheless appeared to have had an effect. They all married within the faith, but most of all their spouses are good people. Deborah and her husband, a former Israëli paratrooper, have become more religiously traditional, attend synagogue and Bible classes, keep kosher, and light Sabbath candles on Friday night, while teaching Ari and Dani, my grandsons, the appropriate prayers. Both young boys worry about the need to eat kosher foods, particularly since they like pepperoni and fast food. Vera and her husband Russell are not religious but celebrate the major Jewish holidays with friends, both Jewish and Christian . . . Marc and his wife Felice are also secular but do celebrate the major Jewish holidays. Our little granddaughter Sarah attends preschool at the local temple. Eddy and I are periodically present at its *Shabbat* programs, when Sarah is the star pupil. Our children are strong supporters of the State of Israël. Proudly, I have four delicious grandchildren. The baby, Alexandra, a year old, is a wee bit young to appreciate her heritage as yet . . . but it's coming. Maman, you would be pleased.

My years in Yenne also had an impact on the family. Eddy believed that my father had been naïve in not leaving France with the family, when the opportunity presented itself, knowing what the Nazis had done to the Jews in Germany. When Vera was in college, World War II was discussed in class. The students were queried whether there were any Holocaust survivors among them. Vera raised her hand.

"What do you mean?" I said, "you are not a survivor. You did not go to concentration camps—"

"Yes," she interrupted indignantly, "I am indeed a child of the Holocaust. You don't know what it did to me every time you were talking about your experiences."

I looked at her, embarrassed and ashamed, never realizing that this retelling might be hurtful.

"What did you feel?" I began softly.

"I felt afraid! It moved me to think that you almost did not make it."

"But I did. I am here!"

"You were lucky . . . and you see, *you* are a survivor and so am I." She was right, of course.

The reaction of Deborah was different: "In our history class, when the Holocaust was discussed, I was kind of proud because you had been part of it and, at the same time, felt burdened by your suffering." Marc related that as a young boy, he was very angry against Europeans and particularly the French, Germans, and Austrians. Later, as I shared with him my memories of the Good Samaritans, he better understood the situation and partially relented. Marc-David still bears ill feeling toward the French.

As time goes on, the realization that I am indeed a Holocaust survivor is increasingly apparent. My story is comparatively a happy one, because the horrors of the camps were not endured, largely due to the efforts of my parents, good luck, and fine and brave Christian people who took considerable risk to protect my family and myself. However, this period left lasting emotional scars and phobias. Trust in other individuals remains very difficult. I am still fearful of the dark and continue to chew my fingernails. (If Maman knew, she would turn in her grave.) I miss her.

Stopping at a red light one morning, driving to work, my father's face appeared, reflected by the rearview mirror of the car before me. Shocked, I stared intensely as if trying to persuade him to look at me, smile, and say, "I am here for you." But there was no smile. It was not him; simply another man who resembled Papa. Such a good friend! I miss him.

On *Yom Kippur*, I attend *Yiskor* memorial services. Although not a religious Jew, I still believe in tradition. Maman always attended these annual services, to pray for lost family. I waited for her outside the synagogue, according to tradition, forbidden to enter because my parents were alive, wondering what was going on within. The mystery is no more; children are allowed in the sanctuary during the Memorial Prayer. My family is with me, remembering their grandparents. At special *Shoah* (Holocaust) remembrances in synagogues worldwide, names of relatives who died in the ghettos and concentration camps of Germany, Poland, Lithuania, and other Eastern European countries are recited. Yellow Stars of David, representing those which identified Jews during the Holocaust, are distributed for the congregation to wear. It is an effort to do so.

*I am the lucky one.* I was meant to be saved so that I could marry Eddy and enjoy my children and grandchildren, in the winter of my life.

Many personal memoirs of the Holocaust have been published. My story is about a childhood which had a profound impact on my Judaism. Historically, anti-Semites perceived Jews as ugly, greedy, dishonest, dirty, and controlling, and subsequently when their monies and property were confiscated, were then considered weak, unable, or unwilling to defend themselves. These representations increased my sense of inferiority. Countering these images were the incredibly courageous Jewish fighters in the Warsaw Ghetto Uprising of April 1943 against overwhelming Nazi forces, and the Jewish participants in many Résistance groups in World War II. Not to be ignored are the inumerable contributions of Jews in music, the arts, sports, science, medicine, journalism, politics, and literature, resulting in many Nobel Prizes and other awards. For about two thousand years, Jews wandered the world without a homeland, usually persecuted. They were expelled from many nations. Israël's statehood, and its subsequent heroic wars of survival, have reversed these misperceptions. Nevertheless, the rise of worldwide anti-Semitism and terrorism place Israël and the Jews once again at risk.

Aix-les-Bains—Monument commemorating
the Resistants who have fallen in combat

Aix-les-Bains—Mont Revard

Madame Thomas

Monsieur Thomas

Yenne 2000—From left to right: Michèle Thomas,
me, and Janine Thomas.

With this memoir, I have crossed the Demarcation Line again, but am now in a true Free Zone. Forever the optimist, I would not otherwise be a survivor! Although childhood in France was most difficult, my native country is still regarded with affection. France provided me with a wonderful education. I love the language, the wit, and its philosophers. After so many years in America, my unquestioned allegiance is to the United States but remain French in background and outlook. As Josephine Baker used to sing: "J'ai deux amours, mon pays et Paris" (I have two loves, my country and Paris).

"Je me sens bien dans ma peau."

Along with many good friends, Jews and non-Jews, I rejoice visiting my beautiful Paris, savoring a fix of *vrai* (real) coffee with *vrais* croissants and *vrai* Brie. I then happily return to the United States, where my heart is. "La vie est belle!" (It's a wonderful life!)

It is liberating now to speak of these remembrances and cathartic to write about them.

They are also a legacy for my children and grandchildren and, in a small way, add to the growing history of the Holocaust, to assure it is not forgotten.

"Never again."

# EPILOGUE

## FULL CIRCLE

In April 2003, three years after our last visit to Yenne, André Chagnon received a letter from Yad Vachem in Jerusalem, informing him that his parents, Marie and Placide Chagnon, had been designated, "Just among the Nations" for having helped Jews during the Occupation, at their own risk and peril. Their names will be engraved in the Wall of Honor in the Garden of the Justs in Yad Vachem. A medal and a diploma of honor in their name will be given to their son during a ceremony organized by an Israëli diplomatic mission.

I was elated and called André to congratulate him. Modestly, he said, "We do not deserve any medals or diplomas. You have the same flesh as I, *la gamine* (the child)."

In the late fall of 2003, Madame Thévenard and, posthumously, Monsieur Thévenard were also honored by Yad Vachem.

March 28, 2004. André is to receive the Yad Vachem Medal today, surrounded by Marcelle, his wife, Janine and Michèle Thomas, Herbert Herz, the representative of Yad Vachem, Ed and myself. André has reluctantly agreed to accept the Yad Vachem decoration, but no way is he going to be subjected to public scrutiny in a town hall ceremony.The venue is a gourmet restaurant near Yenne,:"Le Coq en Velours" (the Velvet Rooster) in St.Genis-sur-Ghiers, well known for its specialty; chicken in wine and cognac flambé, whose spices remain a well kept secret.

After the luncheon, I express my affection and eternal gratitude to André, Michèle and Janine, without whose parents' courage, my family and I almost certainly would not have survived, nor would I now have lovely children and grandchildren. The presentation by Herbert Herz follows. He explains the role of Yad Vachem, speaks of the martyred Jewish children memorialized in a garden at Yad Vachem, and finally:addresses André: 'As the representative of Yad Vachem for the Savoie and Switzerland, and on behalf of the Ambassador of Israel to France, I bestow upon you and your parents, Marie and Placide Chagnon, the Medal of the Righteous and this Certificate." By this time, there is not a dry eye at our table.

André, the man who vehemently opposed the decoration, is thoroughly touched, red-faced, tearful; and very sad, repeatedly examines the medal in its elegant velvet lined box made from the wood of olive-trees and shows it to the pretty young proprietress of the restaurant where he is well known.

It is one of the most uplifting events of my life, poignant, and bittersweet.

In this sorry troubled world, this is a very special moment.

A *Mitzvah*.

Jérusalem, le 23 mars 2003


Réf: CHAGNON PLACIDE & MARIE – FRANCE (9919)


Nous avons le plaisir de vous annoncer que Yad Vashem a décerné le titre de
"Juste parmi les Nations" à Placide et Marie Chagnon, pour avoir aidé, à leurs
risques et périls, des Juifs pourchassés pendant l'Occupation.

Une médaille et un diplôme d'honneur en leur nom seront envoyés à la mission
diplomatique israélienne la plus proche de l'adresse des récipiendaires, qui
organisera une cérémonie en leur honneur. Leurs noms seront gravés sur le Mur
d'Honneur dans le Jardin des Justes parmi les Nations à Yad Vashem,
Jérusalem.

La copie de cette lettre est adressée aux personnes qui ont délivré un
témoignage, ainsi qu'aux autres personnes concernées.

Nous vous serions très reconnaissants de bien vouloir nous adresser, si possible,
une photo de M. et Mme Chagnon, de préférence de l'époque de l'Occupation.

Veuillez agréer l'assurance de mes sentiments les meilleurs.


Dr. Mordecai Paldiel
Directeur du Département des Justes


**Letter from Yad Vachem to André Chagnon**

Monsieur and Madame Chagnon

André Chagnon receiving the certificate from
Herbert Herz of Yad Vachem.

# BIBLIOGRAPHY

I am most grateful to the following authors and institutions for the invaluable information referred to in this memoir.

Robert O. Paxton—*Vichy France*, Old Guard and New Order, 1940–1944—Columbia University Press/New York—1982

Henri Amouroux—*La Grande Histoire des Français sous l'Occupation*—Le Peuple du Désastre-Quarante Millions de Pétainistes—1939–1941—Bouquins, Robert Laffont—1997

Jonathan Fenby—*France on the Brink*—A Great Civilization faces the new Century—Arcade Publishing—New York—1999

Winston S. Churchill—*The Second World War*—The Gathering of the Storm—Houghton Mifflin Co. Boston—1948

Bernard Blumenkranz—*Histoire des Juifs en France*—publiée sous la direction de—Collection Franco-Judaica—Edouard Privat, Editeur—1972

*Quid 1981*—Editions Robert Laffont, S.A., et Sté des Encyclopédies Quid, 6 place, St-Sulpice, 75006 Paris—1980

Serge Klarsfeld—*The Children of Izieu, A Human Tragedy*—Harry N. Abrams, Inc., Publishers, New York—1985

Abraham Rabinovich—*The Battle for Jerusalem*—The Jewish Publication Society—1987

Elie Wiesel—*Memoirs—All Rivers Run to the Sea*—Shocken Books—1995

Edwin Black—*IBM and the Holocaust*—Crown Publishers—2001

*International Jerusalem Post*—No. 7743—Octobrer 2003.

*The Jewish Museum in Paris*

*The Library Archives in Aix-les-Bains and Chambéry.*
*The Museum at Izieu.*

\*    \*    \*

I was not always able to place my recollections in proper chronologic perspective and carried out research to jar my memory in this regard, and to place the events described in historical context for the interest of the reader. Some names in the narrative are fictionalized in order to protect the individuals' privacy, or because they are unknown.

# ENDNOTES

## Chapter I

(1)   *Savoie.* The Savoie has an interesting history dating to pre-
historic times. There is an ethnicity between the people of the
mountains and the Allobroges (Celts of the low country who
were under Roman control). Savoie became an independent
fiefdom which belonged to the Comtes de Savoie in the eleventh
century, who subsequently, became Dukes de Savoie in the
fifteenth century. Geneva was part of the dukedom. In the
nineteenth century, the Duke de Savoie crossed the Alps to
the Piemont and conquered Italy. Turino was then the capital
of Savoie, replacing Chambéry. In 1860, during Garibaldi's
struggle for Italian unification, the Duke became the King of
Savoie and Sardinia, and King of Italy, but Savoie, by a
plebiscite, was now part of France. Early in World War II, the
Nazis placed the Savoie under Italian guardianship, except
for the cities of Lyon and Marseille. *Personal communication*
and *Quid 1981*—p. 850

(2)   *The Demarcation Line.*—*La Grande Histoire des Français sous
l'Occupation*, Henri Amouroux, pp.560–564—*Vichy France,*
Robert O. Paxton, p. 53-54

## Chapter II

(3)   *Pogroms.* The assassination of Alexander II in 1881 triggered
continued pogroms, despite the first democratic revolution,

resulting in a constitution and formation of a *Duma* (Parliament) occurring in the same year. In 1903, the pogrom of Kichinev, one of the worst, was followed by additional pogroms in sixty-six towns and six hundred twenty-six localities and lasted three years. At the outbreak of World War I, there were seven million Jews in the Russian Empire, including Poland (two million), Lithuania or Little Russia, and other Baltic countries.Three hundred thousand Jewish soldiers served in the Russian Army. After the Bolsheviks took power in 1916, the Whites and the Reds took turns in persecuting the Jews in their *Shtetlen* (small Jewish villages) within the Pale Settlement area designated for Jewish inhabitance. By 1917–1921 at least sixty thousand Jews were killed.

*The Jewish Museum in Paris,* June 2000 exhibit

(4) *Hitler.* The defeat of Germany in 1918, the triumph of the French, and the punitive Treaty of Versailles converged to aggravate Hitler's resentment. Marshall Hindenburg, an old man of eighty-three, as chancellor, was the head of the government. Although he was very popular with the masses, big business pressured him towards change and a younger leader, Adolf Hitler, with whom they had allied themselves. The German economy was collapsing, unemployment rose to 2.3 million in the winter of 1930, and the Nazi Party gained the support of the malcontent. In January 1933, Adolf Hitler won the election and assumed the post of Reich Chancellor. *The Second World War—The Gathering Storm,* Winston S. Churchill. pp. 52–65

(5) *Mein Kampf.* Man must fight to exist, and this power to fight depends on purity. The Aryan race is pure. Germany has to rid itself of the Jews who are pacifists, cowards, and not pure. Germans have to be trained to be soldiers. There can be no sentimentality in foreign policy. There is to be expansion to Russia but definitely no alliance with her. *The Second World War—The Gathering Storm,* Winston S. Churchill. pp. 52–65

(6) *Dreyfus*: (1894–1906) Alfred Dreyfus was a French Jewish officer in the high command unjustly convicted of treason and sentenced to hard labor for life, on Devil's Island, French Guyana,. After

ten years and several trials, which received worldwide attention, Dreyfus was exonerated and returned to the army. A vital turning point of this *Affair* was an article written by the writer Emile Zola in *l'Aurore* entitled: "*J'accuse*" which condemned the French Army, as well as the government, for their intolerance, falsification of documents, and perjury.

*Histoire des Juifs en France*—published under the direction of Bernhard Blumenkranz—pp. 351-360; *Quid 1981*—p 771b

(7) *Anti-Semitism* flourished among the nationalist right. Books and articles of this period dealt with subjects such as the *Jewish* conspiracy against the Christians, the *Jewish* invasion, *Jewish* terror, and ritual crime. The famous writer, Paul Claudel, who was general consul in Frankfurt in 1911, indicated that he was France's representative in the capital of international Jewry. In 1929, France also suffered from an economic depression which was preceded and followed by financial scandals involving Jews, such as the Stavisky Affair in 1933, in which an embezzler implicated politicians of the royalist right.

*Histoire des Juifs en France*—published under the direction of Bernhard Blumenkranz—p. 365

*Assimilation of the Jews.* Alfred Berl, one of the administrators of the *Alliance Israëlite Universelle*, was unable to recite the *Kaddish* (Prayer for the Dead) for his father. In 1909, another French *Israelite* stated that Judaism is not a religion, a race, or a nation, or even a misfortune (Heinrich Heine), it is a tradition.

*Histoire des Juifs en France*—published under the direction of Bernhard Blumenkranz—p. 367

# Chapter III

(8) *Lithuania.* In May 1919, Vilna, Lithuania's capital, was taken by the Red Army. Poland annexed it in April 1920. During the following year, both countries fought for the possession of Little Russia, another name for Lithuania, which finally became part of

the Soviet Union. The large Jewish population was caught between the two warring armies, enduring savage retaliations from either combatant.

The Jewish Museum in Paris, June 2000 exhibit Quid 1981— p. 1070

# Chapter V

(9)   Students in France are taught of Les Jours Glorieux in French history. Louis XIV and Napoléon I were considered heroic figures because of their contribution to these Days of Glory. Subsequently, discovering that they had been actual dictators, my perspective of them as men of worth, changed. It was surprising to learn that the Revolution of 1789 was initially fomented by the bourgeoisie but in fact, the actual storming of Versailles and the Bastille was carried out by the people of Paris. The less violent Revolution of 1830 proclaimed freedom of speech and universal suffrage (except for women, however, which was not obtained until 1944). The Revolution of 1848 introduced the word proletariat to the world. The Commune of 1871, during which Parisians ate rats to survive, eventually led to the Third Republic, which lasted until the formation of the Vichy government. These revolutions were passionate, working-class declarations, reaffirming the principles of 1789: Liberté, Egalité, Fraternité ou la Mort. During the 1920s and 1930s the working class became more aware of their power with the ascendance of Karl Marx's communism and the Bolshevik Revolution in Russia. Personal observation

(10)  Front Populaire—Quid 1981—p.776-777

(11)  French virtual civil war—Vichy France, Robert O. Paxton, p. 381

(12)  The Frente Popular in Spain, in the same period, had similar goals to those in France, with the encouragement of the communists while fighting General Franco's fascists during the war, supplying his army weapons and military aircraft. The city of Guernica was bombarded and destroyed by the Germans. This massacre was immortalized by Picasso's famous canvas depicting the carnage. Personal communication

(13) *Congés payés—France on the Brink*—Jonathan Fenby, p. 121

(14) Victor Hugo, in *Les Misérables*, describes similar actions during the short-lived July Revolution of 1830. French history records other similar episodes. In 1937, the workers occupied the factories in order to make their demands known. *Personal observation*

(15) *Anti-Semitism—La Grande Histoire des Français sous l'Occupation*—Henri Amouroux, pp 13-18—*Histoire des Juifs en France*—published under the direction of Bernhard Blumenkranz—p. 180-184

(16) *Munich—La Grande Histoire des Français sous l'Occupation*—Henri Amouroux, pp. 28, 76, 96

(17) *The Maginot Line.* A French fortification extending from Switzerland to the North Sea, in two sections constructed in concrete, steel, and wire. It lacked sufficient canons and observation posts. Most French forces were stationed behind it. It proved uselesss, because the German offensive was directed around it through Belgium. Hitler built a similar fortification called the Siegfried Line which was penetrated by the Allied Forces in 1944-1945.

   *La Grande Histoire des Français sous l'Occupation,* Henri Amouroux, p. 62, 155, 157

# Chapter VI

(18) *Bombardments: La Grande Histoire des Français sous l'Occupation,* Henri Amouroux, pp. 120–123

(19) *Exodus from Paris—La Grande Histoire des Français sous l'Occupation,* Henri Amouroux, pp. 318-341

(20) *Maréchal Philippe Pétain—La Grande Histoire des Français sous l'Occupation,* Henri Amouroux, pp 295-296

(21) *Pierre Laval—Quid*—p. 772

# Chapter VII

(22 ) *Armistice—La Grande Histoire des Français sous l'Occupation,* Henri Amouroux, pp.718-719—pp.436-438, p.586

*Vichy France.* Robert O. Paxton—p.367

(23)  *Life in Paris in the 1940s—La Grande Histoire des Français sous l'Occupation*, Henri Amouroux pp 893-899—pp. 856-858,

# Chapter VIII

(24)  *The Germans invade the Savoie—Library archives—Aix-les-Bains.* June 2000

(25)  *IBM and the Holocaust*—Edwin Black—p. 292-332

(26)  *The Vel d'Hiv' Raid—La Grande Histoire des Français sous l'Occupation*, Henri Amouroux, p. 919

    *Histoire des Juifs en France*—published under the direction of Bernhard Blumenkranz—p. 400

# Chapter IX

(27)  *Yenne not strategically important to Germans—Personal observation*

# Chapter X

(28)  *French Education System—Vichy France.* Robert O. Paxton— pp. 153-160

# Chapter XI

(29)  *SOT and Relève System—Quid p. 779*

    *La Grande Histoire des Français sous l'Occupation*, Henri Amouroux—p.920

(30)  *Maurice Gamelin*: French general who was a witness against Pétain after the war. *Quid 1981*, p.780

(31)  *Edmond Jouhaud*: French general condemned to death after the war, but his sentence was commuted to life imprisonment. Subsequently liberated in 1967—*Quid 1981*, p 1431

(32)  *Edouard Daladier*: prime minister from 1938 to 1940. Imprisoned by Vichy in 1940, deported to Germany from 1943 to 1945,

reelected as a deputy in 1946, and later mayor of Avignon from 1953 to 1958—*Quid 1981*, p.771

(33) *Joseph Darnand*: chief of the milice. Condemned to death and executed in 1945. *Quid 1981*, p.780

(34) *Jacques Doriot*: founder of the Parti Populaire in 1936 and of the newspaper *Le Cri du Peuple*. For a short period, Maurice Thorez' rival for the communist party's leadership.He was believed to be excuted by the Germans. *Quid 1981*, p.780

(35) *Général De Lattre de Tassigny* took part in the invasion of Normandy, and subsequently was involved in the Algerian War and the abortive overthrow of the French government. He died of cancer in 1952.

    *Quid 1981*, pp. 780, 1578

(36) *December 1943*. Formation of the *milice*, a paramilitary police force of about 45.000 volunteers led by Joseph Darnand, Vichy's secretary-general for the maintenance of peace and order, who fought against the *Maquis* and helped enforce the deportation of the Jews.—*Vichy France*, Robert O. Paxton, p. 298

(37) *Devaluation of French money—Personal remembrance*

# Chapter XII

(38) *The Diary of Anne Frank*. A journal written by a young teenage girl who hid with her parents, relatives and friends in the house of non-Jewish acquaintances in Amsterdam, Holland, during World War II. This diary has been reprinted in many languages. The journal was interrupted by her arrest and subsequent death in a concentration camp. *The Diary of Ann Frank*—Ann Frank, Doubleday, a division of Random House,1995

(39) *Paul Touvier*. Head of the milice in Lyon, a subordinate of Klaus Barbie, the Gestapo Chief of the region. After being initially pardoned in 1971, was finally arrested in 1989. He was convicted of murdering Jews and died in prison in 1996.

    *France on the Brink*, Jonathan Fenby, pp. 218–219

*Maurice Papon* had been a senior official at the Préfecture in Bordeaux from 1942 to 1944 and had been involved in the deportation of about 1500 Jews, including 200 children to the concentration camp of Drancy, outside Paris. After the war he became head of the Paris Police under de Gaulle, and a cabinet minister in the government of Giscard d'Estaing. During his trial in 1997-1998, at age 87, he remained unrepentant, considering himself a scapegoat for the nation's guilt, and remains so today, in 2004, while in house detention.

*France on the Brink,* Jonathan Fenby, pp. 210-220

(40) *Alain Mousse* was deported and died in 1943. *Personal communication from the director of Archives in Chambéry,* June 2000

(41) *Klaus Barbie* was the chief of the Lyon Gestapo and called, "The Butcher of Lyon." He executed many prisoners, and tortured some of them himself. He is responsible for the death of the famous Résistance leader Jean Moulin and the deportation of the children of Izieu (ages four to fifteen). After the war, he was recruited by the American authorities for counter-espionage (1947–1951) and then helped to escape with his family to Bolivia where he became a businessman. He was finally extradited in 1983 to stand trial in France. When interrogated about his role in Izieu, unrepentant, he replied, "It was war." In 1987, he was sentenced to life imprisonment *The Museum of Izieu. June 2000*

*The Children of Izieu, A Human Tragedy,* Serge Klarsfeld, pp. 36, 95, 123-127

(42) *Rachel, Exode et Résistance en Savoie.* Rachel Perelstein—1999—Editions Cabedita, La Lechere, CH 1197 Yens-sur-Morges, BP 16, F-74500 Saint-Gingolph

# Chapter XIII

(43) *Resistence: Vichy France,* Robert O. Paxton, pp.293-297—*La Grande Histoire des Français sous l'Occupation,* Henri Amouroux, p. 747-824

(44) *Library archives,* Aix-les-Bains.—June 2000

(45) *Oradour-sur-Glane.* In 1944, in revenge for actions of the Résistance, the SS massacred the population of Oradour-sur-Glane. *La Grande Histoire des Français sous l'Occupation*, Henri Amouroux, p. 943—After the war, twenty-five Germans who participated in the massacre were sentenced to death and prison. *Quid 1981,* p. 1431

(46) *Général Leclerc*, posthumously Maréchal Philipe Leclerc, joined De Gaulle early on, was involved in theAfrican campaigns, the Invasion in Normandy, and the war in Indochina. He died in a plane accident in 1947. *Quid 1981*, p. 781

(47) *German Reprisals—Library archives,* Aix-les-Bains.—June 2000

(48) *End of the war*—The deaths or detention of famous collaborators such as Darnand and Pétain are celebrated in January 1945. Laval, trying to escape to Spain, is caught, attempts suicide in prison, and is executed in September 1945.

*La Grande Histoire des Français sous l'Occupation*, Henri Amouroux, p 954-960

(49) *Denazification*—Although revenge by the deportees is warranted, there apparently are few individuals who take part in such activities, and these consist chiefly of members of the Palestinian Jewish Brigade. The Nuremberg trials and some other legal pocedures, involving criminal physicians and troops taking part in massacres, take place.

*Memoirs—All Rivers Run to the Sea*—Elie Wiesel—p.143

# Chapter XV

(50) *The Mandelbaum Gate.* Named after the owner of a large house that had been destroyed in the 1948 War of Independence and was located at a barricaded street intersection which served as the only crossing point for diplomats and tourists along the Jordan-Israëli border. *The Battle for Jerusalem*, Abraham Rabinovich, p. 30

(51) *Yad Vachem.* Everlasting memorial in Jerusalem established by the government of Israël to the six million Jews murdered in the Holocaust. *Personal Observation*

# Chapter XVI

(52) *Simone Veil.* Jewish author, philosopher, government official. A concentration camp survivor who later converted to Catholicism. *Quid 1981*, p. 717d

  *France on the Brink*—Jonathan Fenby, p. 218

\*    \*    \*